Unreality and Time

SUNY Series in Philosophy
Robert C. Neville, Editor

Unreality
and
Time

Robert S. Brumbaugh

State University of New York Press
Albany, New York

Published by
State University of New York Press, Albany
© 1984 State University of New York

For information, address State University of New York
Press, State University Plaza, Albany, N.Y., 12246

Library of Congress Cataloging in Publication Data

Brumbaugh, Robert Sherrick, 1918–
     Systems and tenses.

     1. Time--Addresses, essays, lectures. I. Title.
BD638.B77   115   82–665
ISBN O–87395–613–3   AACR2
ISBN O–87395–614–1 (pbk.)

10   9   8   7   6   5   4   3   2   1

Contents

Acknowledgements

Portions of this book previously appeared in the following publications. The author gratefully acknowledges the editors permission to reprint them here.

"Kinds of Time: An Excursion in First Philosophy" from *Experience, Existence, and the Good: Essays in Honor of Paul Weiss* ed. I.C. Lieb. Copyright by Southern Illinois Press.

"Metaphysical Presuppositions and the Study of Time" from International Society for the Study of Time, *Proceedings* III, 1978. Copyright 1978 by Springer Verlag.

"Systems, Tenses and Choices" from *The Midwestern Journal of Philosophy*, Spring 1975. Copyright 1975 by Robert S. Brumbaugh

"Applied Metaphysics: Truth and Passing Time," from *The Review of Metaphysics*, 1966. Copyright 1966 by The Review of Metaphysics.

"Plato and the History of Science," from *Studium Generale*, 1961. Copyright 1961 by Springer Verlag.

"Changes of Value Order and Choices in Time," from *Value and Valuation: Essays in Honor of Robert Hartman*. Copyright 1972 by The University of Tennessee Press.

The following publishers have given permission to use extended quotations from copyrighted works:

The Magic Mountai., by Thomas Mann, translated by H.T. Lowe-Porter. Copyright 1939 by Alfred A. Knopf;

The Castle, Definitive Edition, by Franz Kafka, translated by Edwin and Willa Muir, copyright 1941 by Alfred A. Knopf.

Introduction

A S THE TWENTIETH CENTURY moves toward its close, we are in
a position to draw some new conclusions about systems
of philosophy and about the nature of time. These two
topics are closely related, and are in fact causally connected.

My present discussion centers on three points. First, I argue
that there are different kinds of time—different in structure, in
relation to action, in method proper to their observation—and
that a human being can select among them at will. This seems
a remarkable advantage, brought us by the evolution of intelligence and the development of precise language, but it need not
be. For if, as I think is the case, these different time concepts
arise by abstraction, by partial attention to different aspects of
objective situations, mis-selection is always possible. In fact, if
we were to operate without sophistication, assuming one time
scheme to be the best one, the assumption would fail to match
the actual case three times out of four. It is not enough to say
that intelligence uses spatialization, abstraction, or what you
will, to carry out its function: it is more versatile than that, and
its functioning less one-dimensional.

Second, I think that the notion that there can be any *single* nature of time, to which the law of contradiction will apply as it does to substances or flowing qualities, is mistaken. A sign of this is the history of controversy among scientists, philosophers, and artists who tacitly accept the assumption. We are dealing with a complex sequential relationship which will not, as a whole, exhibit any common property of quantity, or quality, or relation, or modality. The assumption that we can find a suitable model, formal or mechanical, to serve as paradigm fails as well. Mathematics, which serves science elegantly, is too firmly committed to a formalist standpoint to accommodate processes of indefiniteness, unwelcome lack of firm borders between cases, or shifts of truth value with change of date. Mechanics is also firmly committed to built-in notions of atomicity, linear causality, and reversibility. (A sign of this is my discovery that when Plato tried to find one mechanical model of time, he—and the Academy— ended up with *four,* and the four were incompatible.) Aesthetics still might offer a hope that by intuition and appreciation, rather than abstraction or manipulation, we can isolate some one quintessential quality. Perhaps, we might think, if we look to metaphor, a single temporal metaphor will emerge. The facts, unfortunately, do not match this expectation. There are a number of alternative and exclusive "root metaphors" applying to temporal thought. And when we look at the qualities of time as it is presented to us by the most sensitive of human observers— poets, musicians, sculptors, film makers—we find the same diversity.

Third, I think that the diverse ways of paying selective attention to temporality are associated with certain natural sensitivities and talents, and certain dominant professional interests, in such a way that one of these ways becomes paramount for each person and profession. By "becomes paramount" I mean that by a generalization to metaphysics, the time structure that seems most natural, sensible, and noticeable is thought of as the *only* "real" structure. It may well be that this selective adoption of temporal orientation offers a partial *genetic* explanation for the diversity of the systems of speculative philosophy, just as those systems offer *formal* and *causal* explanation of the alternative time systems.

In my own exploration, I have used classical concepts. The first is Plato's being-to-becoming hierarchy, schematized in the divided line of *Republic*[6]. To understand what time is on any given level we may do either of two things. We may by generalization move one level higher in the direction of changeless form and eternal order; but this, in the very nature of the operation, loses characteristics of the "time" we set out to explain. Alternatively, we may go from the higher level to temporal phenomena by the addition of increments of unreality. Each such step downward adds a new degree of irregularity, diversity, and nonbeing to pure form. (That the step is "downward" does not mean that it involves a loss of importance: reality, importance, and interest may not correlate exactly.)

The second concept is the distinction of tenses which appears particularly clearly in Plato's *Timaeus* and *Parmenides*, and later is elaborated in logic, cosmology, practice, and metaphysics by Aristotle. In particular, Aristotle's notion of a logic able to handle propositions referring to future contingencies, as an extension of a purer mathematical analytic, proves useful.

Third, there is an Aristotelian rule, that "proximate causes are more explanatory than remote ones," which seems useful and applicable in the present context. In application, it suggests that we will understand time in a more fine-textured way if we see it relating two levels of Plato's hierarchy which are relatively close—e.g., a formal logic with "tenses" and a practical logic with formal connectives — rather than relating two levels farther apart.

Before setting out on more detailed discussion, let me examine these general points in somewhat more detail.

Natural science has always been lucky in its relation to logic and mathematics. Whenever new models were needed—from non-Euclidean geometry to Catastrophe Theory—the formalists had already designed them. This relation does *not* hold between metaphysics and mathematics. In fact, one can see why: the metaphysician must include in his account of all of reality some domains that formalize badly from a mathematician's "timeless" standpoint. If, for example, the metaphysician wants sets with elements that are not completely determinate in having or not having a given property, he must build them for himself. If he wants logical spaces which are continuous traversed from right to left, but discontinuous from left to right, mathematicians reject the whole idea as irrational. If the metaphysician would like a "logic" that captures the formal conditions of positive and negative aesthetic interest, he loses all formalist friends as it becomes clear that "aesthetic contrast" gives an interest value of '1' to '$(p \supset \sim p)$'.[1]

To date, there has been an optimistic assumption shared by metaphysicians and mathematicians that the law of contradiction holds for "time" as it does for substances and qualities. But two thousand years of experiment show that time cannot be consistently treated as a substance, or a homogeneous qualitative stream, or a pure mathematical dimension. It seems that we must recognize time as a complex dynamic relation between realms of being which are very different in kind from one another. In the absence of any suitable mathematical models, we may have to try to find aesthetic and mechanical simile and imagery.[2]

A possible new formal model is an extension of logic suggested by Whitehead's and Sherburne's discussion of "conformal, non-conformal, and partially conformal" verbal propositions.[3] At least, the scheme takes account of alternative "definiteness values" which avoid some of the built-in, and mistaken, notions involved in assuming that logic and mathematics apply to our world in a way that is indifferent to aspects, tenses, or temporal directions of inference. However, the discussion must continue in two directions: one treating time and the practical world, the other time and the aesthetic one. A desk calendar with large spaces exactly illustrates my practical world of "propositions." The calendar I have in mind shows a month at a time, with day and date indicated for each space, and the other months of the year shown in the bottom margin. This is something we take for granted. However, it is interesting to see what happens when we try to generate and construct the "time" and "truth" of the desk calendar from the theoretical pure mathematical and logical components of set theory or formal logic. The calendar simply does not behave properly: there is a slippage here between the theoretic tools and the pragmatic models which proves metaphysically important.[4]

An alternative way of moving from theory to practice is to generate different kinds of time by a Platonic descent. Starting with pure series and pure cycle, we descend through a hierarchy of levels, each of which is created by adding another dimension of unreality, another kind of nonbeing, to the pure and changeless Form of Time with which the journey down began.[5] Even if we can formalize the world of the desk calendar, we must still develop in detail some superimposition of the qualitatively and texturally diverse projections and images of time in art. In literature, for example, we find that often the same author will emphasize different defining qualities of temporality in different works. This is the case with Herman Hesse: *Siddhartha, Steppenwolf,* and *Journey to the East* each concludes with imagery that claims to catch the quality of time.[6] In the first of these, we have reflections in a river as the ferryboat crosses and recrosses. In the second, we have the cold, staccato, fragmented time of the drug-conditioned Magic Theater. In the third, we have a final dry replacement of adventure by written archive, with the exception of one symbolic mobile statue. That statue portrays the gradual absorption of life from the protagonist by the leader who inspired the Eastward Journey. The river and reflection imagery stress the continuity of time; to this, the boat adds a second, rhythmic, regularity across the river's flow. The past persists — though as reflection only — for the boatman. The brittle theater of hallucination stresses vivid discontinuity. Sudden disconnected entries into violent worlds of immediately present possibility produce this framed immediacy. The combination here of vividness, completeness, and disconnectedness characterize this time as what a Whiteheadian would call the "mode of presentational immediacy." The archival transmutation manages a sort of desiccation of present adventure into a world of closed (and dull) atomic items of information in a fixed past, where the referent of a propositon, 'p', is a "fact" of the form 'that p'.

As we have said, metaphysics has been less fortunate than physics in its search for the mathematical models, partly because the study of reality includes more kinds of things, more modes, and more sizes than the mutually congenial domain of physical form encompasses. Qualitative resemblance, for example, is different from logical implication or causal connection. (And still it will not go away, even if we try Aristotle's attempted demolition of metaphor by his definition that "metaphor is calling one thing by the name that belongs to another.") The adventures of organisms, studied in their own scale of space and time, show properties that become too faint to discern if we first dissect them into elements of a wholly different space-time scale.

The study of time is a metaphysical enterprise, not a physical one. The many kinds of succession, inheritance, decision, and aesthetic development demand a more general treatment than a Procrustean hacking into the uniform "moments" of physics. Some years ago, Dr. James Millikan compared what civilization does in its imposition of technological time to midwestern chainstores "cutting up chickens with a bandsaw." The simile carries particular appeal to readers who remember Plato's comparison of the dialectician to the "skilled carver, who cuts at the joints," or even to the modern skilled carver who does the same and serves selectively. (A generation raised in a culture where chicken is thought of as synonymous with "Chicken McNugget" probably will grasp neither Plato's nor Millikan's point.)

Our first attempts at understanding time in itself try naturally to fit it into the models, and approach it with the techniques, we use for the study and explanation of other kinds of things. But it turns out that while every such attempt throws some light on the nature of time, no one of them is satisfactory for philosophic purposes.

I neither think that the question of the nature of time is meaningless, nor that it can be answered within any conceptual model offered to date by Western mathematics, physics, or systematic philosophy. The fact that the mathematicians fail us as an advance patrol is a result of the stubborn preference for pure actuality that animates them; we must try to coerce them into devising formal systems of other kinds. The models of the metaphysician, however, present a different problem. They each assume that time is a substance, process, dimension, or element which is single and to which the law of contradiction applies. Then each examines and generalizes the "time" it accepts as its own paradigmatic case. When the results are mutually inconsistent, it does not occur to anyone at first that this is not an error in observation, but rather one in presupposition. But in fact what we are observing is a complex and heterogeneous collection of four radically different, yet causally interacting ontological domains. Because they overlap, each includes traces and reflections of the others, and this apparent partial homogeneity continues to suggest that all the relevant forms are reducible to some given single basic one. Because they differ, selective generalizations disagree. One may be a metaphysical centrifuge, another a metaphysical deep freeze, that we apply to our investigation, but each is still like a band saw: the results are internally consistent in a way, but fail to make sense in a larger context which includes other devices, observations, and presuppositions.

Chapter 1
Kinds of Time:
An Excursion in First Philosophy

THE TWENTIETH CENTURY is, as everyone knows and says, obsessed with time. In physics, there are variations on the theory of relativity; in biology, the concept of evolution; in technology, the expanding impact of information theory; in astronomy, questions of the cosmic calendar and time scale; in literature, such writers as Joyce, Kafka, Proust, Faulkner, Hesse, Mann (not to mention the more familiar flash-back and fade-out techniques of movies and television); in aesthetics, books on such topics as time and the novel and the dynamics of art; in philosophy, Whitehead on the one hand, Existentialism on the other; and so on.

I want to discuss the nature and measurement of time from a philosophic point of view. First, I will suggest that no specialist's view of time is as general as a metaphysician's. Second, I will argue that the existence of four classical, convincing, and viable analyses of time in metaphysics itself shows that we are dealing with a phenomenon so complex that philosophers to date have only succeeded in grasping separate aspects, not in integrating them to view time in its entirety. Third, I will try to present two problems of modality which are closely related to questions currently central in philosophic speculation, and show the bearing of the nature of time on their solution.

First, then, I want to show that there is no specialized discipline which has an adequate treatment of time, but that the nature of time is a *philosophic* problem. In physics, time is an undefined basic notion. Great complexity of prediction and precision of measurement is introduced as one studies the relative speeds and frequencies of motion in nature. But the use of clocks presupposes the notion of the equality (i.e. the congruence) of successive stretches of time, and so does our judgment of uniform acceleration or motion.[1] The clock pendulum, for example, must take equal time for each arc, if it is to measure as we want it to. And when we want to know whether two time stretches are equal, we must *finally* appeal to psychology: do we feel certain that they are equal? There is no more certain way. (This is not a philosopher's fancy, but a corollary of such scientific treatment as A. Einstein, *The Meaning of Relativity.* —Princeton, 1955, p. 2.)[2] In psychology itself, however, time is often treated by looking for some clock-like mechanism in the brain. An observation that estimates of elapsed time shorten predictably when one has a high fever suggests that there is such a mechanical clock, and also suggests physical explanations for discrepancies sometimes observed between our subjective time estimates and mechanical clocks of other kinds. This is, ultimately, of no use to the present discussion, for psychology goes to physics in these cases to find out whether and which clocks are uniform, which time spans are congruent, and that is exactly the problem physics has just suggested that psychology might explain.

We must then, turn toward aesthetics, and towards some more introspective method of psychology, if we hope for further light. (Towards aesthetics, since it is in the works of art that we may expect to find extremes of dynamics in experience; and also since direct introspection reports must be works of art because they use language to communicate or evoke direct nonsymbolic insight.[3]) And here, immediately, we find a very disturbing thing. In physics, one of the essential postulates we need is that measuring equipment is not altered by its past history (two yardsticks, for example, one heated and the other cooled, will still be congruent when they are returned to the same temperature). But in such a simple aesthetic phenomenon as the meaning or intensity of a repeated refrain or chorus, we find that the previous occurrence has changed the observer's reaction to the repetition: while the poet's refrain is objectively the same line, it has changed its intensity. If this should seem irrelevant to the duration of the poet's line, consider the following simple analogous case: an observer listens to three ticks of a metronome, and then is to say whether the interval is equal between the first and second, and the second and third. Isn't there enough difference in expectation and attitude while he listens for the second tick as opposed to his listening for the third to justify us in wondering, at least, whether his past experience with the metronome (for two ticks) may not alter his judgment of duration and congruence? However elaborately we build measuring mechanisms, when time is being measured we always come back to this sort of thing.

There seems no point in appealing to a common-sense, average, or public time, and dismissing individual variations as impractical or corrigible. Very slight common discrepancies or blurred properties will cumulatively make quite a difference; and public time is a pragmatic construct just as abstract as clock time. When we turn to philosophy, however, it is embarrassing to find not one, but four, classical and viable accounts which claim to synthesize the aspects treated in physics, aesthetics, common sense, and psychology.

1) Classical materialism treats time as consisting of successive, atomic moments which have no, or minimal, duration.[4] This is also Descartes' view, that the world of extension exists in instantaneous states, each of which is annihilated, then recreated by God in the next instant. This is the sort of definition which nicely fits such an experience as listening to successive ticks of a clock, as it jumps along. It will work well for explaining the regular vibrations of much smaller and faster clocks, such as periodically radiating atoms. And that it *can*, at least, square well with the introspective experience of a highly sensitive aesthetic

observer seems clear from the example of Proust. For, psycho-
logically, time in this mode will consist of fixed moments of
experience, and the man of sensitivity, like Proust, may recapture
them, just as they were, in their vivid separateness, as if one
were taking slides from a memory file and looking at them again.
And for many modern purposes, such as cybernetics and information theory, we think of time this way.

2) The Aristotelian view of time as "the number of motion"
misleads a modern reader until he remembers that motions are,
for Aristotle, stages of organic growth.[5] Sequential stages of growing organization are thus the clock or unit proper to this biological sense of time. In genetic psychology, biology, and
educational theory, the applicability of this definition is quite
clear. That it also fits aesthetics is shown by the terrific critical
impact of Aristotle's analysis of the development of a tragedy (in
which the plot "is, as it were, the soul") as analogous to the
growth of any other organism or organization.[6] We might con-
cede this, and still think that in pure physics only the atomic
or vibratory clock can be used or found; but then we recall that
modern cosmology (following an insight that Kant had) extends
the concept of evolution to the question of the age of the universe, sometimes with the corollary that our vibratory clocks
shift in rate as progressive stages of cosmic organization are
attained.[7] And in this case, the atomic is not even the fundamental sort of physical time.

3) The Platonic tradition has been perplexed by, and drawn
many interpretations from, the terse formula that "time is a projected image of eternity."[8] The central agreement within the tradition is, however, that time, like space, is a continuous field
within which such things as paths of motion can be graphically
conceived, and understood by single equations or formulae. This
emphasis on the continuity of a time which is the backdrop for
phenomena that symbolize or act out equations and ideas, seems
to me to fit extremely well with the somewhat uncanny time
sense of Kafka's *Castle* or *Penal Colony*, where there is a deliberate ambiguity of location, and continuous but peculiarly non-
dynamic imagery. In mathematics, which has always been the
Platonist's dominion, such a field concept of time seems the

only normal one; in psychology, if we should talk about a neutral background field of experience, we could be Platonizing too.

4) However, in modern philosophy the field of space-time is thought of more as a locus of dynamic process, and time might best be defined here as shifting directional intensity (plus or minus, a minus being a kind of monotony). The field in modern physics too (unlike the ether or the pure empty space of classical atomic theory) varies dynamically in its properties.[9] Such variations in directed intensity are familiar properties of our psychological experience: close attention stops the clock, so that time seems shortened, but boredom speeds up the mental clock to a rate so much faster than the one on the wall that we feel the wall clock to be infinitely slow. In aesthetics, probably Thomas Mann's treatments of time in the story (not the theoretical discussion) of *The Magic Mountain* are the most technically brilliant direct presentation of such a time of shifting intensity.

Thus, there are four classical theories, exclusive but each applicable to at least some time phenomena in every relevant domain. It seems evident that each of these four is incomplete, rather than that three are simply wrong. Yet in trying to put the four together, modern philosophy encounters two radical problems. The first problem is to determine the mode of location of things in time. When we consider the atomic view, it would seem that each thing must be located in a present state or moment, completely insulated from any other one. But such a view does not, and cannot, explain time's continuity. It was as much because he was baffled by the way in which his memory slides came to be dated and ordered as because he wanted to understand their several natures that Marcel Proust set about recapturing the past. On the other hand, the Platonic field, homogeneous and with a kind of superconductivity, will not explain the differentiation of events and items in physical time. Plato's theorem (which he proves, but also qualifies and supplements) that "everything which exists in time both is older and younger than itself and is becoming both older and younger than itself," suggests a time with too much continuity.[10]

In treating location in space, Whitehead pointed out very cogently that space is a conductor as well as an insulator, and that two things might overlap (i.e. occupy the same place) without being identical. Our problem now is to extend such a concept of modal location to location in time. This must mean, if we are not to lose the phenomena that we are endeavoring to save, that each individual has a kind of temporal center of location in the present, that it is also simultaneously partially located in the past and the future, but that the degree of this extended location tends to decrease as we leave the center. We must, then, accept as true the theorem that each thing grows to be and is older and younger than itself, without carrying the theorem so far that we do what the Neo-Platonic version did, fuse all times together and destroy (spatialize) temporal flow entirely.[11]

The second problem, closely related to this first one, is to recognize and explain the genuine difference in kind between things that are future and those that are past. Past events are, so far as we can tell, fixed, crystallized, and complete; their fixity, indeed, impressed some medieval thinkers so strongly that they held that "God cannot alter what is past." The future, on the other hand, seems to be a still indeterminate field of open possibilities. (Sometimes, in the natural sciences, this is recognized by using a description of the future in the form of an ordered array of differentially probably future states.) Now, on the one hand, no one is wholly satisfied with a theory like that of Hume which denies any reality to the future, and makes our object of thought when we try to refer to it simply a mirror of the past; this suggests an incredible mechanistic determinism. Yet when a thinker like Mead (or, better for the present purpose, George Orwell in *1984*) carries the notion that truth is a function of future confirmability to the point of saying that the past is just what future evidence will convince us was the past, we resist assimilating the past to future.[12] It certainly seems wrong to think that each of us has the prerogative which God was denied by medieval theologians, of changing the past by simply burning a newspaper. A present, it seems, must be a locus of transformation for two realms—future and past—which lie within some common field, but the contents of which differ in kind. But we can see that this does not at all simplify the first problem of understanding how an existent thing lies simultaneously in its future and its past.

What would constitute a solution to these problems depends on what precise features we take as posing them. My own problem would be this: I am certain that the law of identity must hold literally for all reality, and I am convinced that at least some entities have a history—that is, a persisting temporal identity. But then, *A* is identical with *A* must hold whether two *A*'s are ghosts of Christmas past, or of Christmas yet to come. And what is an aspect of *A* is surely not constitutive of the identity of *A*. When *A* is an abstraction, with an eternal aspect, this fact is familiar enough; but for any concrete entity which is an instance of any set of abstractions, the result is a little more surprising. For, insofar as *A* is identical with *A*, it is modally located across the aspects of future-past-present. But as the distance between *A*-present and *A*-distant (plus or minus) increases, it becomes more and more difficult to differentiate *A*-present from any distant *B*, even though *B*-present would clearly be non-identical with *A*. If we take applicability of the law of identity as a distinguishing mark of reality, and that seems a reasonable thing to do, we conclude that for every *A*, either an aspect is not constitutive of the identity of *A*, or *A* is not altogether real. Unreality is not sheer nonentity, but it is evident in the nature of the case that one cannot say what it *really* is.

Since temporal existence is somehow a persistence of identity through change of aspect, it must be the Platonic time which serves as a locus of identity, and as the common field in which these disparate aspects have continuity, mutual relevance, and order. And in our own experiences, we find that time as eternal is the backdrop against which we see ourselves projected, extending from open future possible selves through present creative choice into a single, complete, and irrevocable remembered past.

The virtue of this solution is that we are able to apply a law of identity to time itself, as the common field of finite aspects, and so to have discussion rather than equivocation. The defect is that no reason is given for the modal transformations of identities as they change aspect from possibility to creativity to closed factuality.[13]

Metaphysicians will go on discussing time as long as men have their sense of wonder and of poetry. How can we help looking for some discursive bridge between the restless finitude of transitory things and their unruffled background of reality? This vivid contrast of appearance and eternity is summed up vividly in the poetry of the Zen Buddhist, Bashō:[14]

> The ancient temple pool:
> A frog jumps;
> The sound of water.

Chapter 2

Abstract Pattern
and Concrete Process:
The Interaction of Space and Time

W HITEHEAD'S ACCOUNT of time as process is an analysis of time that highlights the characteristics we find in the world of art.[1] Process is marked by past continuity, irreversibility, creativity, and hence a partially indeterminate future, and a recurrent three-phase pattern. Whitehead developed his view as a recasting of the concepts of modern science; this recasting includes one restriction and one extension.

The restriction is that Whitehead sees a great difference between science, particularly physics, and metaphysics.[2] Physics can become metaphysics by mistaken overgeneralization. When, as was the case in the seventeenth century, selective attention to the quantitative properties of matter in motion produced brilliant results, there was temptation to argue that the reality of physics was the same as the whole of reality. This argument was that matter in motion constitutes reality as a whole, and all other qualities, entities, and aggregates are reducible to these. The eighteenth century, thus tempted, yielded and the generalization of physics to philosophy was accepted. By the nineteenth century, this acceptance not only held on a theoretic level, but it had taken over and been adopted as part of a general "common sense." Whitehead proposed a restriction of the scope of physics: it is indeed marvelously effective in relating the properties to which it pays selective attention, but its attention still is selective.[3]

The extension Whitehead introduces can be thought of as adding other frames of selective attention, complementing physics by emphasis on such other properties as aesthetic quality, ethical responsibility, and metaphysical novelty. It has seemed to me that a simple way of representing this extension is to imagine the "fundamental observers" of special relativity theory replaced by new, "W," observers. The fundamental observer sees only what is physically "real": matter and motion. He has no attention span; his sole function is to register the "now" at which a moving object crosses his line of sight. The "W" observer has a much wider attention span, and transmits more complex reports.[4]

My purpose in this discussion of process is to differentiate the conception of time as process from the alternative notion of time as a dimension—which is what we find in mathematics— and from time as predictable mechanical succession, which is the concept of technology and physics. The difference is radical, and we cannot afford to ignore it, though earlier I spent a good many years of research trying to disprove it.

Whitehead starts with the notion that the smallest units of reality are more like living organisms than like classical material particles. This is accompanied by the claim that there is continuity in nature, so that properties we find on one level have counterparts, though they may be only slight ones, on every other. Thus there must be something like awareness and decision even on the scale of the smallest bits of nature.

One way of imagining the difference between this view and the non-organic one of relativity physics is, as I suggested, to look at the "fundamental observers" of the two schemes. In relativity, the fundamental observer, R, is quality blind. He only observes material objects crossing a line of sight. And his observations are momentary: he does not remember pattern, but only reports transits. In the other scheme, a W observer notices quality as well as quantity, and his observation time can extend to recognize both quantitative and qualitative pattern. So the "instant" observation is replaced by a "slice" of space wide enough to hold a pattern in question.[5]

I do not want to claim too strong an analogy between W observers of different orders of size and sensitivity. On the other hand, in this theory, we ourselves do count as W observers, alike in kind to organisms of other scales. We vary within our own species, in ways that suggest cross-specific types of variation: for example, Whitehead introduced Wordsworth and Shelley as human observers peculiarly responsive to patterns of quality.[6]

One interesting speculative suggestion follows from this proposed analogy of sensitive middle-sized organisms like ourselves and the far less perceptive atomic-scale occasions. This is that the apparent regularity and predictability of such small particles—for example, electrons and protons—may result from the fact that to date we have had to treat them statistically. On the analogy of a city-planner treating traffic flow, we overlook the eccentricity and individuality of the various involved vehicles. It may be, however, that physics today is close to a level of precision at which individuality makes a difference, so that laws, predictions, and causes must be interpreted differently. For example, an apparatus that can detect the decay of 30 individual protons in an underground ocean of carbon tetrachloride is getting close to individual biography. Or is it? This question, whether individuality makes a difference on the elementary particle scale, however theoretically attractive, can only be answered empirically.

Returning to Whitehead with a view to understanding his analysis of sequence and time, we must start with a more detailed look at the "actual occasions" which are the smallest "organisms" in the scheme. Nature on that scale is made up of actual occasions, eternal objects, and patterns. The actual occasions are concrete centers of activity. They grasp and embody the general properties that Whitehead calls "eternal objects." These are properties for possible actualization; they are abstract rather than concrete; and unlike occasions, they can be in many places at once and can repeat literally in different positions in time. To underscore the difference between abstractions and concrete occasions, and to indicate our different ways of knowing the two, Whitehead discusses the sets of properties that the occasions embody in terms of their arrangement in "abstractive hierarchies" and "associated hierarchies."[7]

The picture is a world made up of actual occasions, alpha, beta, etc. These are centers of activity (thus they are unlike standard substances, which persist passively through shifts of attributes), and they grasp, include, project, and transmit complex sets of properties. The properties, apart from these inclusions, are universals of a sort; and we recognize them by an act of abstraction. The relations of properties as they combine, from simple to complex, can be pictured as a set of inverted hierarchies. Suppose the simplest properties that we can isolate as grasped in alpha are a set A, B, C, D . . . These we can call the *base* of the hierarchy: A_____B_____C_____D_____. . . . But these are together in various ways in alpha: there, for example, we can recognize the more complex pairs, A&B and C&D (thus if A is red and B triangularity, alpha may include the complex property "red triangle" in one way or another.)

$$A \qquad B \qquad\qquad\qquad C \qquad D$$
$$A\&B \qquad\qquad\qquad\qquad C\&D$$
$$(A\&B)\ (\&)\ (C\&D)$$

These combinations finally converge at alpha as the concrete vertex. But Whitehead holds that alpha is infinitely complex; that is, that no set of abstractions can add up to a concrete occasion. We are asked to distinguish between the full set of ingredients and relations of alpha, its "associated hierarchy," and the various partial sets of properties we can abstract, various "abrupt hierarchies." The abrupt hierarchies may be complex abstractions but still are finite.

One way in which an occasion holds its associated properties together in space and through time can be described as a pattern. Relations of distance, intensity, and position are involved here. We must think of the occasion as a center of attraction, holding in place about itself various properties which would, without its attraction, fly apart or vanish once more into a world of abstract possibility, perhaps with ghosts left behind. This pattern is a special class of hierarchies, a spatialized class. A city, for example, operates as an actual attracting center of a pattern of suburbs, highways, railroads, and population distributions. It holds them in spatial focus about its own central attraction.[8] One refinement of this model is to distinguish patterns in *logical* space, where any abrupt hierarchy is a case in point, and in *physical* space, where relations are more exclusive and selective.

An occasion is active through time. This means that its constitutive pattern will change in differently chosen slices of space. Such changes for a given occasion constitute a *sequence*. (When, as a limiting case, the change is simply the loss and recapture of an identical pattern, this sequence is vibration.)[9]

Sequences are spatial snapshots of successive patterns: patterns of growth, dissipation, repetition. An interesting relation that apparently holds between central occasions and their peripheral spatial patterns is that if there is a functional connection between successive patterns, it will continue to relate them until there is external interruption or internal explosion. The relation of cities to their population and environment is a case in point. If the attraction of the center weakens, the pattern flies apart; a sequence shows movement from center to suburb. If the central attraction overbalances the spatial properties held apart by distance the country collapses into an unmanageable central city (modern Athens is a case in point).

Processes are sequences of phases that involve reiterations of pattern. Reiteration is a sequence that is not pure repetition: it is like the variation on a theme in music, rather than a simple re-playing of it. A process, with its emergence of pattern in concrete sequence, is always a three-phase affair.[10] Some initial action, encounter, adventure disturbs a given pattern and contributes a forward temporal momentum. This creates instability, and there follows a stage of attempted re-adaptation, perhaps in another configuration, after a part-to-part adjustment. Finally, there is a new closure realized, and this particular event is over: it has passed into "objective immortality," as a past fact that future occasions may grasp and be influenced by. But its own active role in process is over.

A crucial thesis of process philosophy is that all existence in time takes place, for every scale, by these non-reversible patterns of "phases of concrescence." On the scale of a human student, learning moves ahead in the three-phase process. Whitehead insists that genuine (as opposed to mere rote learning) must take place through the "stages" of Romance, Precision, and Generalization. The first of these is a moment of motivation, the second a period of part-by-part discipline, the third a completed sense of mastery. On the scale of a human civilization, the same sequence in time appears as the "ages" of Adventure, Art, and Peace. A new invasion or migration usually starts off the adventure; then, part by part, fine, useful, and political arts and crafts—including forms of commercial enterprise—are stages of advancing stabilization; finally, with a genuine civilization, there comes a high achievement which is the age of peace.[11]

Clearly, for more complex entities, the final stage is not just suddenly over, as it is for the most elementary events. The architecture of a civilization may well outlast its functioning vitality. An episode of rote learning may partially engage the student, without making any concrete contribution—or, indeed, making a negative one—toward developing "depth of individuality." And yet, despite this difference in partial persistence, the phase pattern is the same.

Process is temporal, but not reversible. The reason lies in the radical ontological difference between past, present, and future. The past, which presses against and jolts the present, is a completed chain of links of fact. The present is a location of *selection*. The inherited past must find a new adaptation, via this present selection, among compatible options now available. This selection includes some sort of purposive direction, or at least some impulse toward conservation. (When this is only toward conservation, the result is simply transmission on a level; higher, it may be an aim at the most stable equilibrium; still higher, it becomes the aim of "living better"—a new stability with new aesthetic contrasts and new emergent complex properties.[12] These new properties can be seen as new abstractive hierarchies, which have aesthetic interest.) The future is a field of definite "possibilities," the "eternal objects" available at a given time for selection as increments of the pattern that comes one step forward from the present. (Whitehead does not develop one part of this scheme that seems important, and that I would call attention to by describing the future as a "field." As possibilities lie farther ahead of any given present, they begin to blur and lose their individual distinguishability. Later I will want to mark this by introducing a semi-Aristotelian distinction between "contingency" and sheer "potential possibliity.")

A fine artist is peculiarly aware of the indeterminacy of the phase of "Art." The past constraints of medium and style leave open an adventurous set of new optional possibilities that can be selected from the open future. Aristotle, master critic but not creative artist, still felt this when he wrote that "the [statues of] Hermes and Aphrodite are both present in the [same] stone."

The Whiteheadian analysis of time gives selective attention to several properties that are part of our normal temporal experience, which other accounts ignore. It catches the intuition of temporal irreversibility, of time as process and process as directional. It highlights the intuition we have of the radical difference in mode of being of past fact, present creative decision, and future vision of nearer or more remote relevant possibility. It does justice to our experience of the world as filled with open potentialities for novelty. (In fact, my own extension of Whitehead would be to suggest that what seems pure persistence or repetition on any one scale will turn out rather to be variation, reiteration, and advance on another—when we find the proper tools for observation on that other scale. The "eternal hills" have their phases of violent emergence, cooling, gradual erosion. The decay of protons, if indeed this is experimentally established, will be a longer-range, spectacular, case in point. Whitehead, however, seems rather to have avoided the question as to whether the *statistical repetitions* for large aggregates might always on a different scale appear as *reiteration*.)[13] The time analysis captures the three-phase pattern of creative advance, which as it relates the temporal modes of being, gives the direction and structure to time that we intuitively recognize there.

And yet, some questions remain. It is possible that the emphasis on novelty has under-emphasized the role of pure mathematical forms that give eternal background and order to sequential temporality. It may be that this emphasis overlooks sameness of shorter cycles in the interest of longer-scale differences. Also , it does not treat the precision of mechanical and laser clocks, whose behavior looks like evidence for *repeatability* without reiteration. That behavior, in turn, argues for temporal reversibility on the level of waves and particles, and for a reduction of causality to Aristotelian "efficient causality."

A following chapter will consider in more detail the Platonic theme of time and eternity, in which eternity is not mere wistful possibility; and the relation of the world of pure form to the becoming we have just been describing. A subsequent chapter will consider an Aristotelian type of time, a kind of decision-making in the present, which is the theater of operation of *prudence.* Prudence is unlike fine art, because the open alternatives do not admit arriving at satisfactory decisions by sudden creative bursts of novelty. There is a much tighter demand for conformity and control. (As an example of misplaced creativity in practical policy, Conrad's anarchist who arranged to blow up the Greenwich Meridian as a gesture of social protest is a case in point.)[14]

In the background of our aesthetic appreciation, there is still technology. From Plato's models of time to our marvelous new measuring techniques, mechanical clocks go along with abstract formulas and concrete intuitions. They are uncreative, not alive, less perfect than some ideal of "equable flow"; but without them, if only for contrast, it is hard to see how we could compare a pure dimension, a creative process, a sequential maturity, and a fluctuating subjective intensity as alternative examples of "time."

Just at the moment, with new experiments and hypotheses challenging the standard paradigms of modern physics and cosmology, the "process" scheme may look more attractive than it deserves to. Supposed "creativity" in nature turns out, regularly, to be capable of mechanical explanation. The three-phase pattern of existence sounds like the grandiose rigid schemes of nineteenth century dialectical idealism and dialectical materialism, which fit reality less and less well as history and anthropology learn more and more. The idea of least particles with some vestigial analogue of originality is not only not confirmable—at least as yet—but perhaps not even plausible. Leibniz, after all, thought his smallest units of reality were "swooning monads" with an experience limited to the unextended time-spans of "instantaneous mind" *(mens momentanea)*. Further, it is odd that the whole world of "aggregates," where any individuality is supposed to be cancelled by the fortuitous behavior of large numbers, behaves quite as stolidly as it does. If both process philosophy and the statistical theory of probability are true, there should be occasional freak deviations (though not "miracles") that can't be accounted for by classical efficient causality. (In fact, Plato seems to have thought this was the case. Epicurus certainly thought so. Hume argued that we have no logical reason for saying that it is not. But they are not observed.)

One invariant common to all four types of time is *order*. There may be variations in what is ordered, whether it is continuous or discrete, whether the order is reversible or not, whether it is or is not accompanied by any given kind of causality. And there may be a provision in the study of time for recognizing several orders, in which case increments equal on one scale may not be so on another.

Chapter 3
Physical Images and
Models of Time:
A Classical Collection

W E COME UPON TIME in nature and technology on the level of common sense and practice. In nature what stands out for us is regular periodicity; in arts and crafts, we devise combinations of cycle and linear series.

Most relevant here is the fact that we can build physical models for the measurement of time. Given this, one might think—and some excellent scientists have thought—that such models can also be taken as the definition of time.[1] But here, as with our more concrete intuitions and metaphors, we find alternative calendars and clocks, measuring by different selective mechanical simulations and summations. We might like to select one of these as a standard, and dismiss the rest; but the same problem of selective attention that Whitehead emphasized in his critique of science occurs in any such exclusive selection of time-defining hardware.[2]

Perhaps the clearest case of the dangers of a single mechanical model is the unsuitability of such models to the awareness of psychological "time," for example, the factor of monotony. In social planning, however, whether we are dealing with commuting distances in a city, lecture lengths in an academic schedule, attention spans on sentry duty, what we need to measure is exactly the subjective lapses. And these, as simple observation assures us, do not at all match the sums of equal increments ticked off by car-dashboard, classroom-wall, or army-digital clock.[3]

We need not step so far outside the level of nature and craft to see the problem. Contemporary science and technology offer a dazzling array of models. We are given the periodicity of the earth's rotation; the seasonal cycle; the regular vibration of selected atoms; the cosmic expansion of the universe; the rate of increasing disorder in a specially combined mixture of liquids or gases. Beyond that, of course, we could take biological evolution as our scale; or our own growing older; or some average of a periodic physiological function, such as pulse rate. A watch-and-clock museum, far less wide-reaching, still has a multiplicity of measuring machines. Since different purposes and types of experiments require different measuring models, we find it hard to select a defining measurement of time. Even for practical purposes, the rate of the earth's rotation has to be artificially modified to stay in phase with the atomic clock vibration (though we could, of course, make the correction the other way).

The world of time gadgetry is a fascinating one, where only an inventor or patent examiner could really feel at home in our contemporary scene. I love clocks, and am fascinated by them; but for the wrong reasons—I see them as a mixture of black magic and fine art. Derek Price's history of the clock as descending first to the tower of the cathedral, then sinking to court and courthouse, next the bank and railway station, finally the individual wrist and pocket of each citizen, is a romance I enjoy.[4] I have had the good fortune to admire clocks in Hampton Court, the Wells Cathedral, Ottery St. Mary's, Munich, Prague, and the fine Vienna Clock Museum. This world of clocks viewed as useful mobiles deserves a book of its own. But for the present, my contention is that from the very earliest designing of physical models of time, there are the same alternatives and ambiguities reflected that we find in the philosophical search for final definitions, the search outlined in an earlier chapter.

In a simple classical form, I think we can already see the alternatives open to this project being explored in Plato's Academy. No one had told Plato that his philosophy didn't permit demonstrating the nature of time by reference to proper hardware. Accordingly—in line with his own insight that "understanding something always requires an example" — he set about observing, describing, and in some cases building physical models that could be such "examples" of time.

Only recently have we recognized that this enterprise was part of Plato's work. A fascinating thing about this recovery of models is that there was not one single paradigm, but at least four. Different purposes and contexts seemed to require different "examples," and no single model seemed to do. It is not a coincidence, I think, that the four "time examples" of the Academy respectively attend to the four levels of reality marked off on the Platonic diagram of the Divided Line, in Book 6 of the *Republic.*[5]

Although it may seem overly simple and perhaps somewhat digressive, I offer this classical collection as a case study. Its moral, that the realm of common sense, practice, and everyday imagination contains different and noncombinable models useful to measure and define time, holds even more clearly for later, nonclassical, periods of invention and technology. The later scene, however, is a thousand times more complex in the measures and mechanisms that it offers.[6]

I

The present discussion will concentrate on four Platonic passages which have been supposed to have been written with models in mind. Recent work in the history of science makes it possible to say more definitely that this is the case, and to specify what the probable referents are.

The result is interesting philosophically as well as historically, since the uses we find of specially designed models go directly counter to the traditional interpretations of Plato which characterize his thought as otherworldly and impatient with phenomena. He appears much more in sympathy with modern empirical interests and techniques than any of our standard histories of philosophy would lead us to suppose.

In the twentieth century, Platonists such as A. N. Whitehead have revived Plato's philosophy, but, to make it compatible with modern science, have felt they must revise it. The revisions take the form of weakening Plato's "forms" from actualities to possibilities; difficulties result when we look for objective ethical norms. If, as seems the case, Plato felt himself able to combine the theory of forms with the kind of scientific inquiry which the set of models we will study reflects, it may be that no revision is necessary to synthesize modern science and classical metaphysics, and that the appearance to the contrary results from too one-sided an interpretation of Plato, influenced by the Neo-Platonic tradition.

There is something strangely arresting about the idea of *mechanical models* in the Academy. The reader familiar with Professor Pepper's analysis of philosophy in terms of the "root metaphors" dominant in different systems will recognize the "diagram" and the "machine" as paradigm cases for two ways of thought that seem completely distinct, perhaps totally opposed. Even if we are not thinking explicitly of any classification or symbolism, this juxtaposition "feels" paradoxical. It becomes even more so when we find that the mechanisms built and studied were archetypes of the modern clock; for the status of time has always been one of the questions that sharply divides the Platonic and mechanistic philosophical traditions. The image of a philosopher in front of a chart covered with the equations of invariant cosmic cycles busily adjusting a small orrery has some of the qualities of the superimpositions of small finite beings and a background of eternity that we find in some Japanese *haiku* poetry. What lends peculiar philosophic interest to our image of the equations and mechanical model, and prevents us from dismissing it as simply ironical, is that it is Plato, not Anaximander or Democritus, who is adjusting the little clock in the foreground of the recreated historical tableau. Perhaps, this suggests, we can design our clocks efficiently and still understand what it is they measure. But before we speculate further about this picture, it is necessary to be sure that it represents something that did in fact happen, so that it has a claim to being history, and not an impossible fiction of a romantic imagination.

For each of four passages which have been interpreted as referring to models, I will first summarize the interpretations that seem justified, and the difficulties attaching to them, without introducing very recent history of science material. The result will be seen to be unsatisfactory, because in three cases it is vague, and in the fourth the very reference to a model seems to involve a technological anachronism. It is also unsatisfactory because the usefulness of models seems limited to mythology and static structure, so that if we order them philosophically in terms of the divided line, they occur only on the lowest segment and the third. This suggests a discontinuity between dynamic and structural properties that almost justifies the traditional idea of an antipathy between Platonism and empiricism.

Having presented interpretations in these terms, I will then show some modifications and additions that very recent work in the history of science suggests. The result is both a clarification of the passages in question, and a reinterpretation of their function, which changes the philosophic picture.[7]

II

Until the late 19th century, as we have said, thanks partly to a tradition which put selective emphasis on some Platonic doctrines and passages to the exclusion of others, Platonic "science" was thought of as radically *a priori* and anti-empirical. There can be no doubt that the stress of Plato's program for science was on theory construction rather than observation. But there can be no doubt, either, if one reads entire dialogues uninfluenced by secondary sources, that the Academy had an empirical-experimental aspect. It is the recovery of an interest in details of the world of appearance reflected in the dialogues that seems to be characteristic of our most recent interpretations of Platonism. One must remember that in programmatic passages, Plato often has Socrates overstate his case. For example, there is a long tradition of contempt for technology based on the dismissal of crafts as "servile" in the *Republic*.[8] But that dismissal did not prevent Plato from being one of the most observant and enthusiastic "sidewalk supervisors" in Athens. If we look at his examples from technology which presupposes some familiarity with it, instead of simply repeating Plato's censure of all crafts in the context of an ideal higher education, the result is surprising. I find, offhand, examples from spinning, weaving, carpentry, ore-refining, instrument-making, medicine, eel-fishing, pottery making, architecture, sculpture, scene-painting, minting of coinage, trireme construction, fabric dyeing, and animal husbandry occurring in passages that presuppose some familiarity with them, and that draw on these arts for concrete example necessary to follow a description or argument.[9]

Now, in the matter of the use of models as an adjunct to theory construction, Plato's statements are equivocal, unlike the forthright dismissal of techniques. It is true he stresses the ideal or abstract character of the mathematician's proper models in the *Republic*, but equally true that in the *Timaeus* he insists they are essential adjuncts to any sound study of astronomy (as opposed to astrology), and that in the *Statesman* the "example" is elevated to a very important role in any method of instruction or prudential inquiry.[10] Practice, again, leans more strongly on apparatus than theory might suggest: one thinks offhand of the evident experimental background of the observations on color mixture, the construction of the regular solids (as opposed to a deduction of their purely stereometrical properties), and experiments which presuppose examination of sets of variously curved mirrors (the apparent properties of which are what Plato says they are, even though modern theory says they cannot really be).[11]

Prior to the Academy, there is a tradition of modelbuilding in connection with astronomy, and this, together with the empirical interest which Plato's practice shows, has led some scholars to wonder whether a number of passages were not written with specific concrete models in view or in mind.[12] There are four passages: the Myth of Er in *Republic* 10, the construction of the world-soul in *Timaeus* 32ff., the dismissal of astrology in *Timaeus*

40D., and the myth of cosmic reversal early in the *Statesman*. (To these one could add as footnotes the reference to an Egyptian theory of "parallax" early in the *Timaeus* and the critique of popular astronomy in *Laws* Bk.10.) The problems posed by these passages are, in part, the result of Plato's use of concrete mechanical or technological words, where either a purely scientific or a purely mythical context would make them inappropriate. In the *Statesman* myth, for example, the universe "revolves, resting on the smallest *pivot*"; in the Myth of Er, the souls see the "nested bowls" spun by the Fates; in the creation of the world-soul, God "cuts," "bends," "splits," "rivets," and "tilts" the "bands" of soul-stuff he has mixed in his "bowl." The difficulties of textual explication begin to disappear if we assume that actual models are referred to as an aid to mythological or popular-scientific imagination. For example, the machinery of the Myth of Er was unmanageable until J. A. Stewart suggested that what the souls see, between incarnations, is an accurate scale model of the universe, which Ananke holds in her lap. This suggestion also makes possible the needed mythical fusion of the motif of "threads spun by destiny" and the motion of the universe, reflected in the "hook," the "shaft," "chains," "nested bowls," etc. of the description of the model the souls see. Again, in the *Timaeus*, the stages of creating the world-soul did not make sense until proposed interpretations of "cutting," resting on technological metaphor and the comparison of God to an Athenian craftsman making a bronze model, suggested that it is here we must look for an explanation.[13]

What can we find about the models used by Plato and the Academy? The references strongly suggest that there was not one single privileged apparatus involved, but rather *four*; two were moving, one seems to have been static, and the fourth is highly problematic. Each of these models seems to single out some one relevant phenomenal or structural property for emphasis, and there is no way to imagine one single super-model that can synthesize them.

a) *The Myth of Er.* The most archaic Platonic model is the spindle of destiny. Professor P.-M. Schuhl has suggested that what is in fact referred to is a group of allegorical statues, and a moving device which one of them held; while this is not necessarily correct it *is* true that Plato's description has the character of a tableau of the sort used in mystery initiations, in which the goddesses and spindle would appear. Burnet was sure the model of nested hemispheres was archaic and Pythagorean; Schuhl's study of the antiquity of the "threads of destiny" motif reinforces Burnet's notion, and suggests a possible evolutionary connection of the moving astronomical model from the mechanism and design of a very ancient ancestor of the spinning-wheel.[4] At first, the details of this postulated Platonic model seem quite simple: nested bowls about an adamant shaft are turned in one direction by one of the Fates, touching the outside, in the contrary direction by a second, touching the inside, while the third intermittently gives impulsions in either direction. Great emphasis is placed on the details of the machine: successive lists give the relative sizes, colors, and velocities of the hemispheres. Evidently, like the souls between incarnations, we are meant to derive some moral from the vision. One could start either with the details of the mechanism, and identify their empirical reference, or with its function and metaphysical significance. In view of the fact that no interpreter to date has made much headway with the former approach, let us try the latter. In this connection, note that the "spindle" is an educational device—"the choice is yours," says the prophet who distributes lots, "god is blameless." This can be true only if the souls have had equality of opportunity—opportunity, that is, to realize that the universe is just. And only if the model shows some correspondence between natural law and the form of justice could the lesson be learned.

In this connection, several remarks about the model are in order. (1) In Plato's own time, it was evidently felt to be archaic. The combination of Orphic-Pythagorean motif and detail would tell us this, even if the demonstrated antiquity of the "threads of destiny" metaphor could not be traced. Charles Morris points out (in *Signs, Language and Behavior*) that an archaic diction and imagery helps to make "religious discourse" more effective, a point which, we may suppose, has never been lost on a sensitive inventor of mythology. (2) The only possible rationale that has been found in the mechanical detail is that of a balance of momentum, assuming color to be correlated with mass. The various laws of nines of Cook Wilson, James Adam, and my own, do demonstrate an equilibrium and balance in the model characteristic of any machine made with a rational plan, in which "justice" is reflected by a balance of parts, each with its own identity.[15] (3) The attempt to correlate details of this myth with Eudoxus' hippopede seems, on the face of it, anachronistic, both because the present passage must antedate Eudoxus' astronomical achievement, and because the "widths and rim" in Plato's model do not correspond to the planetary retrogradation which the hippopede is generally supposed to explain. On the other hand, if both a tradition of model-building and a detailed observation of anomalies in planetary motion are presupposed by Eudoxus' sophisticated achievement, there is nothing impossible in supposing the two distinct anomalies, retrogradation and variation in latitude, to be represented, though not yet causally explained, in a pre-Eudoxian model. (4) The transmission of motion between "bowls" involves some apparent mechanical impossibilities. The resultant of forward and retrograde motions would be what Plato says it is if we had some mechanism of "fluid drive," such as cardboard rings floating on water, as Professor Wallis Hamilton of the Northwestern School of Engineering once suggested. *But* nested rigid bowls in contact won't do. (5) No one since Theon of Smyrna, in the 2nd century A.D., has built such a model as this to see what its qualitative properties would be as the erratic impulsions of the "hands of Lachesis" were applied. Subject to reconsideration after we examine the other references to models—which might lead us to something more sophisticated in the way of gear trains or other types of direct drive, of the form tentatively suggested by both Schuhl and Rivaud—one would conclude that the cabinets of the Academy must have housed their own museum of the history of science, in which an archaic model with symbolism and overtones of the spindle of destiny figured. Not that Plato's version had no novelties—as his stress on the colors and sizes would lead one to suspect it had. For the balancing of size and color to illustrate cosmic equilibrium would involve some inferences from color to density, and from density plus velocity to momentum, which are fairly daring leaps either in the history of theodicy or of astronomy.

b)   *The Statesman Myth of Cosmic Reversal.* More puzzling in many ways, though in the same general category, is the model inspiring the *Statesman* myth of cosmic reversal.[16] The reference to turning on the "smallest pivot" ("foot") is the assurance we need that there *was* a model; so is the description of the cosmos storing up potential energy as it rotates in one direction, so that when released it will revolve "of its own power" for a long time in the opposite sense.[17] The "pivot" is peculiarly telling because, in the more technical astronomy of the *Timaeus*, God in his forethought explicitly decides to create a perfectly smooth, spherical cosmos with *no* "feet" or pivots![18] The reason for introducing the myth in context is to show that in our present universe, there is an element of brute fact; to define an ideal statesman will not, therefore, accurately delineate the function and properties of an actual one.[19] Apparently the motions of "the same" and of "the other" which are co-present in the "persuasion by reason of necessity" in the *Timaeus* are isolated here by a temporal fiction.[20] Schuhl's suggested "model" sounds very primitive—any heavy globe on a fixed pivot, suspended by a cable (compare the chain from the hook of the spindle of necessity in the Myth of Er), would store up enought potential energy to unwind for a long time in the opposite sense to that in which we turned the globe. And such a solid globe would seem to match Cicero's description of astronomical models before Archimedes, models such as Plato himself knew.[21] The only vexing detail this leaves unexplained is the statement that necessarily, when the daily revolution of the universe reversed, every inner cycle also began to turn in the opposite sense: for animal life-cycles, this is obviously fantasy, but for its association with astronomical cycles, the suggestion of some more complex system is harder to set aside. Before leaving the *Statesman*, two minor cautionary comments are in order: a) the catastrophic reversals the myth describes correspond exactly with the statements about "parallax" which the Egyptian priests in the *Ti-maeus* tell Solon, but to which nothing in Timaeus' scientific astronomy will correspond; b) the Egyptian priests, or their colleagues in the Near East, no doubt figure in Timaeus' sardonic remark (40D) about "men unable to calculate," who interpret planetary conjunctions and oppositions as "dire portents."[22]

c)   *Timaeus 32ff.: The World-Soul.* The high point of the Academy's collection seems to be the model of concentric metal bands, which the *Timaeus* describes in its account of the fabrication of the world-soul.[23] There seems good reason to believe that this model was equipped with an incised scale, that the described stages of its construction (in spite of the interference of several sets of metaphor, including the "music of the spheres" motif) duplicate the actual steps of a maker of such models, that the resultant model is a static, structural one, and that Cornford was right in using an early modern armillary sphere in his frontispiece to his *Timaeus* commentary to give us an idea of the finished product.[24] The only objections that have been offered to these conclusions rest on (1) the later reference to study of relative planetary motion by visual imitations in the *Timaeus*, and (2) on the supposed description of some oscillating motion of the central earth when the cosmos (i.e., the metal model of the cosmos?) is in motion.[25] To the first point, it seems an adequate answer to say that the later reference to moving visible imitations is necessary just because the earlier structural model was inadequate. The second point is more complex, and introduces several possible interpretations. Rivaud suggests that if there were a moving model, with concentric tubular shafts driving the planetary circles and passing through the earth in the center, their motion would set up an "oscillation" or "vibration" which Plato may describe. Or we might connect an up-and-down slide of the earth with the "parallax" of Egyptian folklore. Or we might, if we were Aristotle, insist that the earth is in fact rotating in the opposite direction to the cosmic all, at equal speed, which is why it appears stationary—giving it a contrary proper motion to overcome an assumed transmitted daily revolution. Or, in some way, we might connect Plato's "is globed about the axis" with the fact that in later orreries the earth is a sphere, not of metal, but of ivory or clay—so that God must turn it (as He earlier did the body of the cosmos) exactly smooth, and engage in the potter's as well as the bronze-smith's art in fashioning a world.[26]

In any case, the function of this model is to show the simplicity of the structure of reality. Our preference for simplicity in theory matches God's preference for small integral ratio in structure when He geometrizes.[27] Some anomalies are bypassed in this Platonic first approximation—retrogradation is put down to a kind of autonomous exercise of volition by the planets, and the period of Saturn is apparently rather roughly rounded off to 27. Rivaud's notion of a model in motion would, from the evidence given, seem to require a level of technology beyond that of the God who makes the model from bronze bands, and, further, to be unnecessary for the model so made to serve its intended function.[28]

Summary a-c. This survey leaves us in a peculiar position. The technical terms Plato uses certainly suggest intended mechanical referents, real or imaginable. But it is hard to see how a reader outside of the Academy would have known what these referents were.[29] And no passages have ever been cited to show that Plato's contemporaries had any such technological skill as the more elaborate of the proposed models would require.

There is also a certain philosophical disappointment in this reconstruction: we would hope, given the premise that a set of mechanical devices were used to explain cosmology, that they would show some continuity through the four levels of explanation represented by the divided line of *Republic* 6. The reader will recall that the lowest of these types of knowledge is hearsay—folklore, myth, and so on; the second is the recognition of causal sequences of natural phenomena, which is the basis of practical judgment and technique; the third is the level of abstract law and formal structure, which explains why the causal sequences repeat; the fourth is an over-arching concept of value, known as the basis of both logic and nature, by reference to which both consistency and truth are finally determined.[30]

But the *Republic* 10 and *Statesman* passages, in the absence of any ground for positing a setting of technological sophistication, both fall on the level of *eikasia*, while the static metal band model of *Timaeus* 32 is a highly abstract representation of structure on the level of *dianoia*; and thus there is no continuity of model-types which could represent a bridging of the gulf between being and becoming.

d)   *Timaeus 40D.* As against these vague or static mechanisms of folklore which we can only reconstruct in dim outline from the materials used so far, and which we cannot show in any case to have been familiar to Plato's intended readers, *Timaeus* 40D seems at first to hint at something quite different. If we accept the text favored by A. E. Taylor and A. Rivaud, Plato here says that a proper scientific (as opposed to superstitious astrological) study of planetary oppositions and conjunctions must proceed with the help of visible imitations.[31] This reference suggests a scale model that will move, and one in which moving components have speeds analogous to those of planetary motion. But we get no clue as to how this will be done; and a look at the technological limitations of the machine designs of Heron of Alexandria, about two centuries later, makes one doubt whether Plato could have envisaged any mechanism for a model accurate enough to serve this intended function.[32] Can we construe the present sentence differently? Since mythological language replaces the technological metaphors in the *Timaeus* account as God introduces time into the cosmos, and since the pure astronomy of *Republic* 7 uses the heavens themselves as "imitations" of the subject-matter it studies, there would be some reason to expect Plato to say that there is no point in discussing these details without a clear view of the heavens themselves, regarded as imitations of a mathematical system of circular motions. This sense could be approximated if a different text with almost equally strong mss authority were followed. But what spoils the attempt completely is that the complex Platonic sentence is not about abstract equations, but describes successive moments of an actual choric dance. There is no need, with Taylor, to explain its complexity as a result of parenthetical afterthoughts, if we recognize it as such a choreographic description. But imitations of such a visualized planetary dance at once suggest exactly the kind of "model" which the lack of evidence of adequate technology leads one to doubt as the intended referent.

III

One reason for re-examining these passages referring to models at the present time is, as I have said, the relevance of new discoveries in the history of science, particularly the work of Professor Derek Price on the clock and the sundial.[33] As against the vague and tentative conclusions offered above, his findings suggest much more interesting and specific probabilities. Behind the construction of self-moving water-driven celestial globes, and even more the elaborately geared astronomical computers, which had developed by the first century B.C., there must lie a considerable tradition of technology and "proto-clock" building.[34] From Heron of Alexandria, we find out something about the mechanical resources available in the second century B.C., and from the pseudo-Aristotelian *Mechanica* we see some devices of a century or so earlier. But the Antikythera mechanism gives precise evidence of fine mechanical skill, far exceeding that shown in the Heron and Archimedes texts. One interesting conclusion is that the literature of a classical age may completely fail to record or mention highly developed elements of its everyday technology. One must keep this finding in mind in estimating the technological resources at the Academy's disposal.

Now, if Plato's passages had been written a century or so later, we could easily identify the *Statesman*'s reversible celestial globe with the weight-and-water operated "town clocks" which Professor Price describes in the articles cited in note 34. That identification would, from a philosophic point of view, have two advantages. In the first place, it would, by reinterpreting the reference in the "myth of cosmic reversal" as an allusion reminding the reader of the clock in the agora, avoid any notion of an esoteric apparatus familiar only to the circle of the Academy. In the second place, following out the idea developed above that different cosmic models emphasize features relevant to each level of the "divided line," it would put this *Statesman* model just where we want it: on the level of *pistis*, the common-sense world of technology and familiar operational definition. And every reader who had seen the "clock" we are postulating would recognize the reference to its "pivot," and would have an intuitive picture of "cosmic reversal" from remembering or imagining the globe spinning backwards as it was "re-wound" periodically (probably daily).[35] This makes one think that the *Statesman* passage is not only consistent with, but also some confirmation of, the suggestion that ancestors, at least, of such float-and-water-driven, celestial globe "proto-clocks" were familiar in the agora in Plato's own time. This suggests a very precise interpretation of Plato's passage, even to the moment of oscillation as the universe comes to the end of its reverse cycle, and hesitates before revolving in the opposite sense. If within the near future klepsydra wells in the Athenian agora can be dated as prior to 367 B.C., we will be able to supply accurate diagrams and illustrations for future editions of Plato's *Statesman*.

Similarly, Professor Price has suggested, in his seminar, that the *Timaeus* metal band model would be recognized by a reader as the sort of globe of metal bands, held by a statue, that was often, at a later date, another feature of thet marketplace. This model was a descendant of the earlier sundial, designed particularly, as the former also now seems to have been, to mark seasons, solstices, and equinoxes by its shadows. How far that evolution had gone by Plato's time is an interesting question. But in this case, unlike the *Statesman*, the Platonic passage may seem to be somewhat more modified from its proposed proto-clock referent, in its stress on the pure mathematics built into the physical sphere.

A further suggestion comes from working back from Heron's automatic theater to pseudo-Aristotelian, Aristotelian, and Platonic references to self-moving dolls and marionettes.[36] It is clear from these references that, at the very least, weight-and-windlass and direct-drive devices were known in Plato's time which could have been adapted to the moving of astronomical models. And, if we follow Schuhl's explorations, from the opposite historical direction, of the evolution of the Myth of Er machine, the spindle surely carried with it the idea of a model in motion.[37] This last is a peculiarly provocative model. Professor Price, reasoning that Eudoxus' work presupposes a tradition of observation and earlier approximation, has suggested that the "widths of rims" might represent aberrations in latitude, anomalies distinct from retrogradation. In that case a direct-drive device may have kept the intended world-machine in motion. I myself am undecided still as to the balance in this passage of mechanism and mythology. The moral of the myth requires (1) evidence of balance in the various visible details of the model, and (2) some moral lesson (see the *Epinomis* for its explicit statement) to the effect that not even Mars can persist or succeed in a choice to go against the momentum of the entire system.[38] (This comparison with the *Epinomis* suggests that Burnet was right in his final decision to keep "more than that of the others" in the text as a qualification of Mars' retrogradation.)[39] I am quite sure that Plato was visualizing a variation on some archaic cosmic model as he wrote; but I still am inclined to believe that this mythical machine may have an equally mythical mechanism. On the other hand, it does seem likely that there was a continuous evolution among pre-Eudoxian models, and that the two anomalies of deviation in latitude and retrogradation had been (at least approximately) observed and distinguished as phenomena which astronomers recognized before they had theories or models adequate to explain or duplicate them.

For the model to be used in studying planetary oppositions and conjunctions, if the *Timaeus* 40D citation refers to any actual model at all, we have suggested that nothing less than a moving device with gearing or direct drive duplicating the ratios of astronomical periods would be helpful. (This same idea is evident in Rivaud's proposed mechanism, which he believes would synthesize the present passage and 32C.) But for any model of this type, including Rivaud's tubular housings and shafts, we have noted that we can find no evidence in classical literature that such a device was within or even near the reach of technology in Plato's day. This is where the evidence of the "Antikythera machine" becomes relevant to the solution. Behind that com-

plex device of 65 B.C., there must have been centuries of technological development. This may not have reached back as far
as the fourth century B.C., but, as we have seen, when we compare the mechanism itself with the roughly contemporary literature of engineering, we can prove that a culture may have a
high development of technology which leaves no record in its
literary productions. This means that the argument from our
ignorance of any classical technology adequate to building a
moving model of the present kind has less weight than one
would otherwise have thought, and need not be a serious objection to the existence of the "models" of Taylor and Rivaud.

IV

This material from the history of science helps to resolve some
standing problems in the four Platonic passages we have ex-
amined. In particular, it gives us illustration to accompany the
Statesman passage; it shows that the objection offered above
against believing *Timaeus* 40D to refer to any constructible model
has little weight; it gives us the family-tree of cosmic models
that we need to relate *Timaeus* 32 to the later armillary sphere;
and it opens a new set of possibilities for the explanation of the
Myth of Er. Neatly enough, the outcome now is a set of four
models emphasizing properties that form a continuous series
ascending the levels of the divided line. Their arrangement in
this order suggests that the model of *Timaeus* 32 has as its
primary function not, as has usually been thought, the capture
of cosmic structure, but rather the exhibition of the sensitivity
of cosmic order to a principle of value.[40] In confirmation, we
may notice that the moving model of *Timaeus* 40D, used as an
aid to such a "mathematical astronomy" as *Republic* 7 envisages,
offers a much more adequate descriptive analogue of the world's
dynamic structure.

The proposed classification of reconstructed models and the
relevant properties they emphasize is the following:

Table 3.1.

Divided Line	Relevant Property	Platonic Passage
Nous	Value	*Timaeus 32ff.*
Dianoia	Structure	*Timaeus 40D*
Pistis	Physical operation	*Statesman*
Eikasia	Mythological projection	Republic 10

I conclude that the study of Platonic passages and the study of the history of science have an unexpected amount in common; precisely how much, only future archaeology and future textual explication can finally tell. For the modern philosopher, however, the point of most importance is not the recovery of the meaning of "foot" or "retrogradation" in this or that textual passage, but rather the revelation of the compatibility in Plato's mind of the supposed other-worldly, mystical theory of forms and a sharp-eyed, technologically alert appreciation of this world and of scientific empiricism.

Chapter 4
Passage: A Descent into Unreality

Each type of temporal sequence can (and in fact can only) be measured and described by comparison and contrast with an order closer to the "pure dimension" and "simple ratio" of mathematical time. Bergson's contention that intelligence and flow lie at exactly opposite metaphysical poles is precisely what is anticipated by this Platonic observation.[1]

The Neo-Platonic analysis of this is recounted as a history. It is a story of the fall of the soul from light to darkness, one to many, eternity to temporal individuality. Each level may remember the one above it, and feel a longing to return. Each level, by its own nature and without effort, generates the one below it by "overflow," or "emanation." The desire to return is what we feel in our periodic sense of alienation, of homesickness for a unity beyond change. But the human soul can also see its reflection in matter, in its body. If it, like Narcissus, falls in love with that reflection and that body, there is another, greater, fall. Many incarnations may be needed to return to the illumination of the incorporeal light.[2]

The Neo-Platonists also believe that Plato—in the *Parmenides*—has already drawn the road map of this descent from The One to individuality in time.[3] Those steps proceed exactly as the four Platonic models of time, discussed in the previous chapter, illustrate them. There is the world of pure mathematics, the "concordant ratios" in pure mind (projected into Plato's bronze structure of frozen motion in harmonic ratio). There is the world of Nature, the system alike of the stars and of our town clocks imitating their periodic motion. There is the world of individuality, of myth, adventure, and fine art—with its mobile sculptures of spinning speeds, patterns, and colors.

But Neo-Platonism tends to transform Plato into myth, where a modern interpreter would like pure and applied mathematics better. My own interpretation will take the form of tracing the successive departures from the pure number series through its descent into less orderly levels of temporality. The pure series, at each step, takes on a new sort of irregularity, but, until near the end, without losing the topological properties of the eternal order.[4]

This "topological" description is a metaphor. It is as if the exact soul-stuff scale created by Plato's God the Craftsman were elastic, so that it could be stretched and bent; and also could be spun in a privileged forward direction. The individual circles, souls, and motions of subjective time—mythical or psychological—are even more twisted and irreversible in their direction. Thus each level represents a bending, stretching, or spin added to the level above it.[5] To understand or describe "time" of any sort leads, by a sort abstraction, to recognition that there is a participation relation between it and its own more stable counterpart one level higher. It requires a background of Being and a foreground scale projecting the category of the Same to recognize a sequence as Other; whether other in respect to a noncongruent "increment" relation, an asymmetrical "causal connection" between successive terms, or a cyclic modular series as the linear scale is "bent into a circle."[6]

There is, however, another side to this Platonic demonstration. Granted that time presupposes eternity, natural sequence geometry, art the arithmetic of meter and scale: yet the *identifi-*

cation of the vagaries of sequence and successor relation with the pure abstract series of integers misses a crucial point. That identification does, perhaps tell us "what time *really* is." But, if so, it answers a question we asked badly. What we wanted to know was not the eternal Platonic Form of Time. For that is related to participating *times* exactly as the temporal and aesthetic instantiations of the other "real" forms are to their timeless, nonindividual archtypes.[7]

The *understanding* of time which we achieve by correcting the deviations of the Creator's perfect scale requires another operation. We must, by a creative intuition, add a new concrete association of quality, substance, a new jet of nonbeing, to this eternal form. To understand Time requires not only the road of reason that leads from fantasy to eternity, but the constructive appreciation and creation that lead from eternity to concrescence—to adventure, art, and peace; romance, discipline, mastery; encounter, selective adaptation, objective immortality.

In other contexts, I have traced these Platonic levels for a different purpose. That purpose has been to show that the study of language is not a useful route to the understanding of time. The reason is that language manages to cut as well as stretch and bend, and its segments are too arbitrarily detached from the scale to correlate with it.[8]

The Creator's scale can be bent into circles, stretched, and spun. These changes keep its connectedness and the order of its terms, with some projected counterpart of the quality of its increments (for example, the relation of "between" will still apply). We can understand cosmic time, biological time, psychological time, and mechanical time as modifications of the basic scale and cycle. But, as I have said, language manages to cut out pieces, move them about, and so arbitrarily transpose direction, sequence, and order. No single functional relation need connect these snipped-out segments with the closed, rational cycles from which they have been arbitrarily taken.

Number theory is Queen of the Sciences. It involves the concepts of odd, even, prime, and composite number, with the notion of various classes of factors. It also includes the idea of base and modulus, which may well have originally been a theoretical generalization from music.[9]

Pure astronomy in Plato's ideal curriculum is a theoretical deduction of patterns of circular periodic motion—so a study of modular numbers of periods—from more general premises of harmonics and aesthetics.[10] The initial axioms can be collected by bringing together passages from several dialogues.

1)   Of all motions, the circular is the most perfect. Thus,

1a)   A God designing a Cosmos would give it a system of circular motions.

1b)   And, as a theorem of astronomy, Plato explicitly includes the proposition that the speeds of motion of the concentric circles are exactly proportional to their distances from the center.

2)   Of all numerical ratios, those of 1,2,3, and their powers are the simplest; the simplest ratios are most aesthetically pleasant; a God building a system of concentric orbit-rings, or nested spheres, would adjust their speeds to these. The speeds and distances should both show this simplicity.

3)   Time is created by placing visible "markers" in the concentric orbits of the dynamic system. Human observation of these gives us our sense of number, our measurement of periods, and "our tools for research into the nature of the universe."

4)   In a different sense, this applies to the periodic behavior of living systems. Animals are like the cosmos in having periodic patterns—from heartbeats to lifecycles. But the periods for these beings are *epicycles*: individuals wear out, and are replaced by the succeeding generation, which repeats the same pattern.[11] Plato explains this as an interaction between a linear time in which organs and tissues break and wear down, and a cyclical time in which the constant living cycle of the world is "imitated" by the finite animals. This "time" cannot be completely deduced from pure mathematics (though the epicycle still can); it has a direction, modality, and definition of "equal increments" that are different from pure geometry and pure astronomy.

5)   On the level of the part-to-part interactions of inorganic physical elements, the Platonist, following Plato, recognizes a sort of linear, mechanical series that can count as an artificial

sort of "time." Any regular vibration can be seen as a case in point; so can any one-directional sequence of transfer of momentum. It is the intersection of these mechanical series with the self-regulating biological cycles that results in organisms growing older, introducing time as age.[12]

6) The combination of linear and cyclic "time" falls in the domain of "applied astronomy" (in Plato's sense of astronomy as a formal discipline), just as the abacus and money-changing tables fall in the domain of "applied number theory." Here we find the entire apparatus of town clock, calendar, sundial, courtroom water clock. Like ourselves, these artifacts for the measurement of time are a mixture of the circle and the line. Each has its cycle; but its cycles can, in each case, be numbered and ordered against a larger linear background of other "tools for the telling of time." Thus the six-minute courtroom water clock is refilled and linearly counted one hundred times for an official Athenian legal day; that day just matches one rotation of the town clock in the Agora.[13] Ninety days, with moderate deviations, are the periods of the seasons marked out in repeating cycle by the sundial. Four seasons, linearly ordered, is the one-year period of the calendar. For the student of the stars, this is a single unit in a longer period of celestial cycle, perhaps a 216-year period, or one longer. A classical thinker would, of course, like to find some closed largest cycle.[14] But the very relation of *dianoia* and *aisthesis* prevents such a final match of abstraction and observation. Plato had one period of at least 24,300 years; by Roman times one of his commentators is reported to have thought the smallest maximum period must be 33 trillion.[15] This is the point at which we cross the border between science and opinion, reality and appearance, time as kinetic theory and time as linear mechanism.[16]

In the world of nature, where we deal with organic things (including societies which are quasi-organic), time is very different from the pure system of "chronogeometry." Growth is directional, not reversible. Its increments of maturity, of attainment of form, are unequal when we plot them on either a cosmic or mechanical clock and calendar scale. Repetitions are no longer the self-identical eternal cycles of mathematical astronomy, nor the successive yet totally invariant cycles of classical cosmology. Instead, as we have noted, we are dealing with epicycles, in which a given pattern recurs, but in successive individuals. An ontological difference separates the past, present, and future of passage, so that the neat one-modal systems of mathematics and logic do not strictly apply.[17]

In this world of nature, to coordinate activities and to describe change, we introduce a multiplicity of dead mechanical devices. But the behavior of clock and sundial is much closer to the nonbehavioral sequence of the mathematical time series than is the behavior of living animals, evolving species, developing civilizations. Actually, this apparent absolute stability of measurement by mechanisms is accidental. Viewed on another scale, the apparent permanences of the eternal hills or unchanging constellations are in fact processes, seemingly cyclic on a shorter scale, perhaps linear on another. But relative to our own sizes, life-spans, sensations, and projects, these clocks offer a needed, stable background pattern.[18]

As far as human biological time goes, society has pretty well decided what chronological ages will count as marking new equal increments of "maturity." They follow a classical "law of sevens." Medicine is full of more detailed studies of growth and age.[19]

But while lifetimes are variable plotted against mechanical or mathematical measure, they are stability itself when we compare them to the fluctuating impulses of subjective, "psychological" time. This, too, is one-directional. But its elements of successive experience vary eccentrically even when we measure it against the increments of biology. The qualitative structure of subjective time can be described as a succession of "states" separated by "events." The "event" is a discontinuity of some kind; the "state," a persistent pattern of development, or stable quality. Perhaps a more subtle way of treating the structure of this sort of time would be to equate it with Whitehead's "phases of concrescence." On that pattern, as we have seen, each event marks an initial phase of encounter; there is a period of adjustment; then the "state" marks an attained completeness, a relative stability. It is an interesting accident—perhaps one with survival value—

that human memory tends to reorganize our actual experience into the simpler, two-phase, event-state dichotomy.

By the time we have reached this level of our exploration, however, structure projected as quantity, or even as relation, is less important and intrusive than the categories of quality and modality. In the earlier discussion of systems and aesthetic intuition, we mentioned some case studies of the capture of temporal quality in literature. To show that my examples are not an eccentric selection, let me note a few more cases of literary "amplification" of selected qualitative properties of time.

The way in which experience is organized, stored in memory, recalled, and past time-spans compared is complex and interesting. A very general model seemed to me earlier to be one of "states," uninterrupted sequences, separated by contrasting "events." More accurate recent work suggests that when we recall, then re-store past memories there are changes in the remembered time dimemsion of the structure.[20] There must be an objective possibility of noticing some event marking off a state, but there is no necessity, apparently, that a given human observer will recognize just that cut. Thus, though the sequence remains intact, increments of subjective experience will vary drastically (against a mechanical clock), both for a person's experience and between different people whose "objective" shared experience one would have thought was "the same."

A second characteristic of subjective time seems related to modality. This is reflected in the habitual imagination of time series as over, or in progress, or still open to control. This correlates closely, I am sure, with types of normal and of abnormal "personality." It adds one other dimension of deviation to the fluctuating imagined sequences of psychological, subjective "time." In literary time handling, J. Borges has extraordinary virtuosity. His "Garden of the Forking Paths" creates a world that exactly matches, in literature, S. Körner's I* logic in science. More impressive still is Borges's compression of time, the staccato monogrammed imagery, which condenses what could have been nineteenth-century novels into eight-page essays. Or, again, W. Faulkner's *The Sound and the Fury* is a remarkable virtuoso work. What is most remarkable is not the way he sees the space and time of the world through the eyes of the idiot Benjy. It is rather the way in which he shows the future refracting back into a present, as we see what *will* come (with Quentin's suicide, after he breaks his watch, then leaves it for repair, at Harvard). Kazantzakis was a student of Bergson. It is therefore not surprising that in *Zorba*, Bergsonian notions of intuition and of time become incarnate in his characters. The Boss, student of Buddhism; Zorba, passionately overflowing with the inceptive spirit, the present dance; the retrospective Madame Hortense; the heroic, yet normal, absent Friend—these are a series of such incarnations of various types analyzed in Bergson's *Introduction to Metaphysics, Time and Free Will,* and *Two Sources of Morality and Religion.* An anthology of science fiction, R. Silverberg's *Voyagers in Time* is rather a negative than a positive contribution. His authors work out a series of quantitative structural variations which are sterotyped and predictable. (With one exception: the planet where time rate varies drastically with latitude and time direction reverses at the pole.) H. Hesse's *Journey to the East* is, structurally, a remarkable progression of disintegration, from Adventure to Archive. It reminds me of Plato's *Parmenides* read as a literary work, and I am still not sure I have an intuitive grasp, from the inside, of either.[21]

One might have supposed—as I think most of us do unconsciously suppose—that since time of the cyclic type is both the "public time" we regulate our lives by and the "exact time" of the sciences, that both common sense and ordinary language would have a good deal to tell us about it. But they do not, and closer reflection shows that they do not for a very good pragmatic reason.

A human language that always took an absolute, objective "now" as its standpoint would also have to keep its tenses or aspects oriented to the single, objective "past," "present," and "future" which that "now" defines. But inquiry, storytelling, planning, and imagination all involve a shift between the "now" which their statements assume as reference point and the unique now which is the objective present of the speaker or reader. If I am to appreciate or learn from history, for example, I must have a "historical present" orientation: that is, I must be able to describe and imagine myself in a past situation with that past having the modal character it did have when it was present. And in my planning, a kind of future perfect tense, though it may be a metaphysical absurdity, is an absolute practical necessity.[22] One needs this to set out means-ends sequences and indicate what at each stage will, and what will not, still be open to reconsideration and control.

The upshot of this is that whether a given language uses a straight "tense" or an "aspect" system for the time component of its verbs, it must usually be impossible to tell whether the *actual now* of the speaker matches the *linguistic now* of his statements. I can describe the trial of Socrates as though I were present, and discuss tomorrow's picnic as though it were already over and a fact in the past.

This "open" frame is, I believe, essential to human cooperation and survival; but it is fatal to any attempt to understand and describe passage in ordinary language. For by taking different linguistic roles, I manage to treat present, future, and past with any degree of distance and direction I choose, and this suggests only a static series of entities or events preserving their identities quite indifferent to the passage of time.[23]

The syntax of language, in other words, is an elastic gossamer net. It has *no* correlation with objective sequence and structure; it serves primarily, so far as time is concerned, to permit us to act out various subjective scenarios. Thus, while every sentence contains its own "now" as its internal standpoint, and that "now" can be taken as a modal cut between a "past" and "future," and its standpoint can be assumed as $t0$. Language, therefore, in sentences dealing with time, allows each sentence to be its own imaginary world; it lacks even the constraints of "subjective" time. For subjective time does conserve a "chronological" order of "before" and "after," giving its state-event patterns a privileged direction.[24] Linguistic time does not. For example, as novelist writing about the trial of Socrates, I can write "tomorrow is the crucial day!" As actor, dramatizing Plato's *Apology*, I can introduce my part: "Now, I stand before you, a jury of Athenians." As historian, I say "there is no doubt that the trial of Socrates took place in 399 B.C." Here, finally, it is only within a given arbitrary context that one can find any forms of passage.[25] And, naturally enough, we try to correct this by *semantic* rather than *syntactic* correlations, which anchor our sentences to some more "real" temporal orientation. (*What* we mean to say, *when* [by watch and date] we make an assertion, *whether* we are "reporting" or "imagining.")

Finally, at the very edge of pure unreality, we come upon "time" as a sheer succession of isolated moments or static spatial states.[26] Such flashing, evanescent points and lines fall outside of any "passing time" order, just as the numerically identical recurring cycle does on its higher level of reality. Since the postulated moments have no internal connection, neither induction nor causality can be accounted for in a world composed of such instantaneous points of time. But neither can order and succession.[27] We must presuppose or add an idea of continuity, and a memory with imagination, to give us a field in which such instants can be related in a sequential order. And at this point, the investigation has come full circle: for moments placed in this extended field, numbered as though they were determinate, recapture the identification of time with the number series with which our descent began. The main difference is that our moments now lack the internal relatedness which gave points on a line and integers in a series a nonarbitrary order.[28]

The conclusion of this investigation is what a Platonist would expect. On each level, the pure formal order is further modified. With cyclic time, it moves from the one-mode extended number series to a recurring cycle that is bimodal; with "passing time," it becomes trimodal and one-directional; until, finally, on the level of language, an *arbitrary* "now" divides the nonuniform and private subjective states and events which serve as its measure.

To "*understand*" any given level, we must contrast it to a higher level of the hierarchy. Experience or subjective time makes sense when contrasted to growth and public time; public time is an asymmetrical modification of pure cyclic time; cyclic time requires an atemporal, extended background of eternity for its comprehension. What I have tried to do is to indicate how the unchanging form of time mixes with nonbeing to produce the several imperfect series in which time passes, series that our reason cannot help rejecting as unreal. Our own existence, immersed in becoming, shares this same admixture of unreality; and this descent to Plato's cave is the only way *for us* to understand the peculiar nature of physical, biological, psychological, and, most Protean of all, linguistic time.[29]

Chapter 5
Propositions:
Cosmology, Formal Logic, and Beyond

I

THERE IS A GAP between being and becoming that neither formalism nor intuitionism can bridge. Plato, having defended being against becoming, and compared the state of philosophy to a war of gods and giants, finally conceded becoming a kind of reality. (But it is a kind other than, and irreducible to, the "real reality" possessed by the world of form.) Two millennia later, Whitehead presented a somewhat similar qualification in his several treatments of propositions.[1]

Whitehead's formal logic in his and Russell's *Principia Mathematica* treats the timeless formal relations of abstract structure. Metaphysically, this is a "realm of possibility," which is objective, determinate, and unchanging. (Thus, for example, an algebra of 1 and 0 is completely adequate for the "calculus" that describes the truth relations of propositions which refer to this domain.) The language of this formal logic is a symbolism of variables and functions which refers to abstract, formally invariant, entities and their relations. Thus the 'x' in '(x) P (x) ⊃ Q(x)' is a timeless variable, ranging over concrete entities only insofar as they instantiate an abstract unified and property-supporting structure.[2]

But in his cosmology, in *Process and Reality*, for example, Whitehead takes another view. "Propositions" as considered here assert something about an ingression of abstract forms from the realm of possibility as predicates entering the actual occasions in space and time which are their subjects.[3] When the asserted S-P relation holds in fact, the proposition is said to be "conformal." But actual occasions change their relations to abstract possibilities with time: and so the postulated constant truth values of the propositions of formal logic do not match the values of conformality.[4] Some possibilities are, at a given place and time, partially but not wholly ingressive; and so propositions of cosmology no longer obey the exclusive two-value pattern of formal logical algebra.[5]

A further difference arises from the fact that actual occasions act on each other causally through space and time.[6] This means that in cosmology a transitive and asymmetrical relation of causal connection must be provided in addition to the connectives of formal logic (such as material implication, biconditionality, and strict implication).

The perfect model for Whitehead's cosmological logic is not a truth table (not even a table that admits "fractional" values), but a large desk calendar with successive dated spaces, day of the week columns, and entered happenings—past, present, and proposed.

It seems at first to the formalist that with a sufficiently fine-textured apparatus, he can generate the "desk calendar" logic from pure formal entities and relations.[7] This is a special case of the attempt to create existence from a collection of essences, or concrete entities from sets of abstract ones. But the history of philosophy offers an impressive consensus of experimenters who discover that this cannot be done. (The one alleged exception, Plotinus, has been misread on this point. In V. 9.12, he admits forms indefinite in complexity, so that finally each may match only one existent instance. But he denies that there is a form for a concrete individual, e.g., Socrates.[8])

Abstraction and formalization involve replacing one kind of time by another.

The converse attempt, to treat pure logic and mathematics as techniques of temporal construction, fares no better. In fact, from Plato on, it has seemed clear that there is a total difference between mathematical insight and proof and the auxiliary tools of mathematical experimentation and construction. Plato's *Theaetetus* shows that standard models of thought as psychological process — blank tablets, impressions on wax, birds in an aviary — can never reach the necessity and universality of the simplest proven mathematical theorems. For example, there is no possible *experimental* proof in any finite time that there is one and just one even prime number.[9] The causal relations of procedures are not the formal deductive relations of ideas. And the attempt to reduce logic to inquiry and mathematics to imaginative carpentry loses the connectedness, often far from obvious, and the precision that give mathematics and formal logic their value. (See, on this point, Russell's chapter on Dewey in his *History of Western Philosophy*).[10]

The simple and tempting assumption that one of these frames of reference can be substituted for the other is a mistake. What it does is to treat as interchangeable two sorts of "time" which are mutually irreducible.

Whitehead also envisaged a further kind of logic — an "aesthetic" one — more general than the precise but abstract tool of mathematics and the more concrete but more contingent "proposition" of cosmology.[11] Presumably, since "contrast" is a key term in Whitehead's aesthetics, there will be a sequential "contrast" relation of two entities, x and y, which fails to be an analogue of the law of contradiction. (That is, to take the simplest case, if x is a substance with one property, P, and x is subject to a rule of aesthetic contrast (implies aesthetically,' $\supset^{aes}$', will represent this), $P(x) \supset^{aes} {\sim}P(x)$ will follow. We will return to this later.[12]

II

From the standpoint of formalism, a description of the ordinary time pictured by my desktop engagement calendar is an incredibly complex enterprise. I have worked on various large

tables of "fractional truth values" and "partially conformal propositions" trying to isolate the simple patterns that go into everyday planning. Instead of trying again to generate a formal
description of everyday happenings from elements carefully
purified of any "happening" quality, I will start with the calendar
and the world it reflects.[13]

Calendars come in various designs, and these may bring out
different patterns selectively. But in general the calendar consists
of numbered spaces, its dates, in which can be written brief
abstract descriptions of happenings. If one is fond of logic, it
makes sense to think of the squares as subjects of propositions,
the noted happenings as predicates that do or do not attach to
them. Thus "March 21—dentist" describes a positive connection
of date and dental visit.

The first thing I note, as I look at the calendar, is today's date.
I check each day as it passes, and the set of checks stops at
March 20. This means that all the earlier March notations are
facts (or nonfacts), not engagements. Thus, "March 12—dentist"
either does or does not refer to an actual visit. (If it does, I may
want to say it has a value of 1, meaning that it did happen; if
not, that it has a value of 0, that it didn't happen.)

Now almost all standard logic presupposes a world where all
calendar entries have values of either 0 or 1, regardless of the
relation of today's date to any "subject" date. Thus "March 12—
R, dentist" states a fact, and in the standard interpretation, this
has always been a factual (= 1) statement (the dentist visit having,
presumably, *always* been a predicate attaching to this date). But
my calendar does not work that way: "March 21—R. to dentist"
is not, now, a fact—nor a nonfact, either.[14]

Rather, that entry is an engagement: I am saving time for it,
and it is therefore real enough to exclude other options for 10
A.M. on the calendar. Obviously, though, it is not completely a
fact: I am still present in my desk chair, not in a future dentist's
office. Yet it is partially definite: if there were not already a set
of conditions satisfied — such as an appointment, a convenient
schedule, and indeed an actual dentist — I wouldn't regard this
as an *option* (which takes up the 10 A.M. spot) but at best as a

"possibility." A possibility in this sense is a kind of floating event with no definite, actual connection to a date. So, on my calendar, I find for a day next week: "12:30—lunch try Hatsune?, 12:30—check to bank?, 12:30—sherry Saybrook?" As weekends are more remote, the possibilities noted become more and more extensive: "Vermont?; soccer at Storrs?; to New York, galleries?"

Now the obvious thing about this practical patterning of time, and the thing that gives fits to clearheaded theorists, is the peculiar status of the "options." Only a classical theology or a physical science impervious to common sense could assert that tomorrow's appointment has the same factual status as the one I kept yesterday. (Try to use next year's proposed charitable gifts for current tax deduction!) So any system that assumes that options and facts are the same starts with an assumption that is pragmatically unworkable.

But it doesn't work well, either, to assume an exhaustive division of all events into facts or mere possibilities. The dental appointment tomorrow is already partially determinate: it excludes other engagements, and as it gets closer, the exclusion is more firm and the encounter more nearly complete. This is like the patterns of biological growth, with increments of definiteness added to the coming event. In the case of growth, however, successive increments move toward definite mature form, rather than toward a given temporal occasion.[15]

Oddly enough, this fact—of the partially determinate status of options—is overlooked or underestimated by some of our everyday institutions. Reservations, for example, assume that I *do* take the 8:03 plane to Tampa—in which case I am billed for the flight—or that I *do not*, in which case I have received no service, and have no bill. Now it would certainly be absurd to charge cash for wholly unanchored possibilities. But I can't help thinking it is foolish to act as though my reservation were no more definite ten minutes before takeoff than it was ten weeks before.

Compare this situation to an early British court ruling on a charge of criminal attempt. A would-be assassin missed the duke and drove his dagger into the chair back instead. The court acquitted the attacker, opening its ruling with the statement "For where was the harm?...".[16] Subsequently, however, the law has decided that "harm" is not such a one-or-nothing metaphysical entity. Neither is an "option."

It isn't hard to design a logic for describing patterns of calendar time. (But it is not a project that mathematicians and logicians would undertake without strong urging.) For the *past* dates, we need only two "values," 1 and 0; each entry either did happen as noted or it did not. For the marginal possibilities, noted but with no precise time attached, a value of $\neq 1$ seems a fair description: these are less than definitely the case, and indeed some of them may not be "really" possible — given the other facts and engagements entered on the calendar. Where 1 and 0 are exclusive values, $\neq 1$ and $\neq 0$ are not: I could (possibly) go to Vermont Saturday, but I could (as far as things stand now) go to Hartford. When a value doesn't hold, I can represent this by a "not" or minus sign $(-)$. So a value of -1 is $\neq 1$, and one of -0 is $\neq 0$. In standard formal logic, this is simplified by the fact that 1 and 0 are the only values the logician recognizes in his system. But for the practical planner, there are more values and relations. Thus if a given entry is not a fact (i.e., if it is -1, or $\neq 1$), it may be wholly nonexistent $(=0)$ or partly, but not wholly, realized as yet $(\neq 0$ and $\neq 1)$. (Note that since "possibilities" are simply descriptions of events not attached to definite dates and places, they include situations where there is yet *no* degree of determination of the possibility in question.) This means that "things that are not facts" are not a single set. The domain includes past things that did not happen; but it also includes future events that as yet have no definite toehold in space and time.[17]

The most interesting calendar items are the future options, the $\neq 0$ entries. As I approach the dentist's office at 10 A.M. on March 21, my dental appointment is not past; it is not a completed fact. But it is not, either, some simple daydream in wide margins of desk calendars. (The entry "will not need dentistry" in the March top margin is indeed such a daydream; it is an $= 0$, $\neq 1$ entry.)

The rest of the present chapter will offer *formal* analyses of facts, possibilities, and options, as a supplement to my present rather plodding practical examples.[18]

III

Your first reaction to the phrase "applied metaphysics" is likely to be the same as Glaucon's when, in *Republic* VII, Socrates mentions "solid geometry": "But, Socrates, this science hasn't been invented yet!" I agree; and my present discussion is an argument in favor of its invention. Ideas, such as the idea of applying knowledge of principles to practical situations, have peculiar adventures in history. They have to wait offstage until they are discovered, that is, until there is an entrance cue; and the importance of the onstage role has nothing to do with the length of the pre-entrance wait. For example, the industrial revolution could have occurred in second century A.D. Alexandria.[19] There was complex gearing, there were treatises on mechanical advantage via wheel and lever, there was steampower, smiths could make sound boilers. It is all well, and partly true, to say that slavery was responsible for the absence of any impetus toward a modern industrial use of invention; but the more important fact is, that the *idea* of applied science had not yet been discovered and institutionalized in the West. The great designers spent their time working out plans for an automatic puppet theatre and self-propelled windup toys.[20] Just as there was no such idea of applied science then, it seems to me that we have no idea of applied metaphysics today. There is no doubt—as sporadic adventures have shown—that philosophic principles as abstruse as Hegelian dialectic can have tremendous practical impact and power. But the translation from principle to practice is unsystematic, a diffusion by accident; there is no disciplined attention to the sort of application which leads from pure science to practical invention.

Whitehead's brilliant analysis of the problems of the modern world concluded, you will recall, that our century is one in which progress and welfare require—and require to an unprecedented degree—redesign of our basic inherited "common sense" conceptions. We are trapped and hindered in our thought and planning by unrealistic and outmoded notions: of location, of duration, of education, of social progress, of beauty, of religion. I am convinced that he was right; but how many of us have thought about the implications of his criticism of simple location toward, for instance, the designs and types of maps that we use in textbooks for our elementary schools? We have not seen the need for sustained attention to this sort of problem.[21]

One sign that the idea of applied philosophy is still unappreciated and not realized is to be found simply by looking at a Sunday paper. *The New York Times* has experts and editors for Religion, Sports, Science, Education, Fashion, and Law—but it has no Philosophy editor, and most rarely does a reporter see anything of public interest to be said about the meetings, lives, and opinions of eminent philosophers. Governments and corporations are not advertising for consulting metaphysicians in the press, though if they only knew it, they desperately need them.

There are two reasons for our failure to develop and explain the applications of metaphysics. The first is our conviction that our proper job is to get principles clear; the translations and middle terms needed to make those principles effective are left to shift for themselves. The second reason is that we have an unrealistic idea of what application should do. We have the illusion sometimes—at least some of us have had it—that since we see general principles more clearly than unthoughtful experts in the practical, we are also better at their own work than they. This is the wrong notion of "application." Principles, as I will show, do not lead deductively to specific and unique practical actions, but to the discovery of new limits, new directions, and new programs of exploration.

IV

As an example of applied metaphysics, I will, for the remainder of my discussion, focus on the twentieth-century discovery that time is not like space, but a passage and transformation between modally distinct past and future. This is a good case study for my purposes for two reasons. First, because the practical relevance of the idea is fairly evident: I will indicate this for religion, logic, psychology, and education.[22] Second, because the idea has been common currency among philosophers since the turn of the century, and the failure to apply it illustrates exactly what I have in mind when I say that we have not yet really discovered the *idea* of metaphysics in application. My main attention will not be to the technical aspect of the concept of passage, but rather to the middle terms which can act catalytically to show the implications of the idea for problems and procedures in other areas of specialization than our own.[23]

We will start by accepting the insight that time involves a change of modalities as it passes. This means that there is a genuine ontological difference in the kind and the definiteness of being which past facts, present options, and future possibilities possess. Part of this difference can be summarized by the assertion that *there are no past possibilities, and there are no future facts.* It follows that we have created an unreal problem in our uncriticized assumption that the concepts of causation, truth, law, and determinism, which hold elegantly for the factual past domain, must also apply to the future. That past time is a fair sample of all time is a mistaken metaphysical assumption. (That it is an *assumption* was argued most persuasively by Hume; that it is a *mistaken assumption* by Bergson.)[24] Determinism does hold for the past, but if we were not committed to notions of verifiability, truth, and fact which are all past-oriented, it would be evident from our own immediate experience that it does not necessarily follow that such determinism also holds for present or future.

This insight, once it is really grasped, can help on the most immediate level to resolve one of the most prevalent of our current human perplexities. We find and teach that there are rigorous causal laws in nature, and also in the behavior of society, which an individual is unable to evade, escape, or alter. On the other hand, we are frequently aware—or made so by court and school when we are not—that we ought not to have acted as we did in a given situation. The more intelligent one is, the more intolerable the problem seems: God, or the law court, or some super-ego holds us accountable for what we ought to do; and yet, the more we understand and analyze our past behavior, the clearer it seems that we could not have acted in any way other than we did. In a more sharply focused situation, this is often the dilemma of a criminal court: expert testimony by psychiatry and sociology seems increasingly able to show that the criminal, in that situation, could not have resisted behaving as he did; but the judge and jury insist that he is responsible for a wrong deliberate past choice. This dilemma is the result, I hold, of ignoring the difference between the past as it was when it was present, and as it now is, crystallized into adamant causal chains forged by necessity. Looking backward, we will never "observe" past open alternatives: every antecedent will have had one and only one causally related consequent.[25] But this past was once a present moment in which looking forward showed no "future facts," fatalistically deployed, but rather showed relevant alternatives, among which there was opportunity for selection.[26] The Kantian nightmare of an agent with a sense of responsibility caught in a universe of blind, inexorable machinery results from a confused time sense in the dream.

It would be a digression to argue that each of Kant's *Critiques* is exact in its description of one aspect of reality, and that each describes one and only one of the three modalities of time. It is not digressive to point out that, without the problematical hope of the third critique, Kant's view of the human self caught in the natural order is in fact what I have called it—a nightmare, resulting from the time confusions in our dream. Nor is it digressing from my main point to add that our present educational system is doing everything it can to make the tension more acute and the dream more incomprehensible. We are doing an increasingly brisk, precise job in secondary school science of demonstrating the case for a world of fact that admits no glimmer of caprice, freedom, or chance in its causal order. We are doing an increasingly more crucial job in awakening awareness of responsibility in our students. Sometimes they feel this responsibility toward society, sometimes toward their own authenticity. We are doing nothing at all to explain this schizophrenic change in the conception of reality that varies with each move between classrooms. We are upset by the attempts our students make to retain more intellectual integrity: by apathy, by indiscriminate activism, by distrust of an intelligence and authority that has set them a puzzle they must solve, with pieces that *cannot* (and I mean cannot) be fitted together into any solution. They are not too young to learn that it is the difference in time which produces the apparent contradiction; they are not too stupid to understand this; but we are not wise enough to tell them. This is my first case study of the need for an application to a vital current problem of an abstruse metaphysical principle.

As a second case, the recognition of this modal character of time has implications for logic that are necessary but perhaps not welcome. Logic, traditionally, is concerned with propositions: propositions refer to states or facts. In "Aristotelian" logic or in Tarski, the correspondence of proposition and referent is definitely the case, or definitely not.[27] And the truth-value remains the same, regardless of the date. But one part of our new discovery about time was stated in the formula that *there are no future facts*. This means that there are cases—those, namely, of propositions with future time-reference—in which the meaning is definite enough, but the truth is only fractional. A "choice now open" or a "possibility" has *some* ontological status; it is not a pure Parmenidean nonentity.[28] It therefore also has *some*, though indefinite, correspondence with the propositions asserted about it. If our patterns of thought are to match the patterns of life, our logics must be modified to include indefinite "values." For example, a four valued scheme of 1, 0, $\neq 1$, $\neq 0$ may be needed to distinguish the degrees of definiteness in the correspondence of assertion to reality. And, in *sharp distinction to nearly all antecedent formal systems*, those values are in some cases going to change with the relative dates of assertion and reference of the propositions. Otherwise, we perpetuate the illusion that there are future facts, that time is like space, that nothing is lost in translating a problem or decision that confronts us in the present into a language which allows no other modes of existence than the eternal and the past.

Once we have applied our knowledge of the nature of passing time to the reform of education and the reconstruction of logic, we can turn to a third enterprise. This is not an awakening from a dream nor a better-honing of a blade for Ockham's razor, but the criticism of an ideal construct common in the West to religion, theology, physical science, and some recent developments in psychology. Whether it was Plato's fault (as Heidegger believes) or not, the paradigm case of "knowledge" was taken in the West to be the geometric diagram.[29] Add to this the multiplication table, the geographical map, and the taxonomic chart, and we have the material for a mistaken ideal construct of a being that knows everything. The ideal is formed by combining our pleasure in those facts that fit neatly in chart and map, with a rejection of the uncertainty that attaches to areas not so neatly charted. Now, such an ideal knower is useful for various theoretic and expressive purposes and is used in many ways. The most striking cases, of course, are the three major religions of the West, which, in trying to express a profound religious intuition, attribute omniscience to a supreme being. Omiscience is then defined as perfectly determinate, non-temporal knowledge of "all things," present, future, or past, on the model of the scholar whose map shows him "all the cities of men," north, south, east, or west. I have no quarrel with the intuition expressed, or with the doctrine of omniscience as an analogical mode of its expression. But I do want to point out that omniscience can only mean "knowing everything that there is to be known," and since time is unlike space, there are no future facts for any being to know.[30] Too literal an interpretation of a powerful insight has led to the dilemma of a God who foreknows the future, creates a world in which that foreknown detailed plan will necessarily unfold, and then judges individuals innocent or guilty as a result of choices for which God holds them responsible. The tension is barely tolerable; in the end, the religious vision may be more compelling than the logical and ethical problem it brings with it, and, as with St. Augustine, the doctrine is accepted—though not understood—in the interest of the vision. But it seems to me wrong to insist that true faith rest on acceptance of a metaphysical absurdity. Two ways are open for our further search for understanding here. The first, explored by Whitehead, Hartshorne, and Weiss, has a divine mind and divine knowledge cognizant of, hence changing with, passing time. The second way, which should not offend anyone familiar with past discussions of the sense in which words apply to human and divine attributes, is to see and say clearly that "knowledge" as understood in past discussions of omniscience is used in an eminent sense, and, as applied to God, must go beyond and be quite other than the literal anthropomorphic scholar with his pen and map. Whatever this eminent omniscience may be, it need not be incompatible with human responsibility and freedom. The same objection applies to the scientist's ideal of Laplace's demon or angel: given the state of all matter at an instant, this hypothetical superior mind can calculate every future fact and date it. This notion, too, is a construct that ignores the difference between space and time; its assumption of future facts, determined but simply inscrutable to ourselves, is quite inconsistent with notions of purpose and responsibility, including the behavior of the scientist himself. Whitehead has made the point so well in the first chapter of *The Function of Reason* that I have nothing to add here.[31] On a more specific empirical level, not only does our knowledge of time require reconsideration of the divine in theology, of the demonic in Laplacian demonology (or angelology), but of the human in parapsychology. Claimed cases of precognition, that is, of a vision in full factual detail of future events which the agent himself does not then proceed to bring about, though this claim has been accepted from the time of the youth of Aristotle, must rest on a misinterpretation of the evidence at hand. As an applied metaphysician, my function is to raise questions and start discussion of the implications of basic principles, not to confuse my role with that of the expert in theology, statistics, or extra-normal psychology; so on this point I will say no more.[32]

V

I have been exploring the implications of the fact that time has different modalities.[33] I now intend to turn to a second aspect of our discovery that time is not like another spatial dimension. Any sequence of events in which there is a series of ordered increments of transformation from remotely possible to actually attainable to actual is a case of passing time. There are only four kinds of such series that I recognize as distinctive types: vibration, growth, pure extension, and sequences of subjective experience in memory and anticipation. But the public time, clock-time, which we construct to synchronize our private ventures and lives with those of others is only one of four. There is considerable convenience in correlating a "time" series with some uniform motion in space; the main advantage, I suppose, is that we can use spatial techniques to show what the "successive equal increments" are, and measure their "extension." But there is a total metaphysical error involved in proceeding to assume that this particular type of series, that of public time, is uniquely real, or objective, or identical for everyone.

As a matter of fact, time in nature and in art is a series of successive realizations of increments of maturity or of completed form. Here ordinary language (which lets us down completely in most discussions of temporality) has already recognized that there are successive equal increments of human maturity. These are not equal projected against the calendar; growth has a different structural plan. (If we trust ordinary speech here, it tends to mark out increments that are *logarithmic functions* of equal calendar units.) But our habit of assuming that a given five minutes is "the same length of time for everyone" has led to overlooking obvious indications that it is nothing of the sort, and as a result to serious practical mistakes.

These mistakes are of three kinds: wrong ethical judgments between generations that disrupt human harmony, wrong factual judgments of four distinct types that inhibit personal effectiveness, wrong notions of our own control of temporality that lead us to cheat ourselves of longevity.

Once we recognize that growth takes place at a rate that slows down with age when we use the calendar as its measure, we can also recognize that the rate of experience and the resulting "length" and "shortness" of given clock periods must also change. Aristotle remarked that a child on the second day of its life *doubles* its total number of increments of experience; to do this for the man at the "height of his intellectual powers" (which Aristotle set at 49, in a passage written when he was about 49 years old) would require 17,795 times as long. Yet Aristotle goes on, in the irascible spirit of all adult custodians of children, to describe them as deprived adults, deficient by nature in temperance, patience, attention-span, and understanding of their elders. (For example, Archytas had invented a new baby rattle; Plato, unmarried and childless, admired it because it began to teach rhythm and mathematics earlier; Aristotle thought its more important virtue was that it kept children from breaking up the furniture, "since young things cannot be still."[34]) The fact is that time is not the same length for everyone; it correlates at a different rate with increments of boredom or activity per tick of the clock. I can wait patiently in the dentist's office, with the serene virtue of an adult attaining the years of full intellectual perfection, for a quarter of an hour. But my daughter Joanna is a distracting companion. "It seems forever"; "It's been an awfully long time"; "Let's play another game now." This shows, it seems to a right-thinking parent, that children just are not as disciplined, well-organized, or patient as we are; their memories are not objective, either—Joanna tells her mother that our short wait "took forever," which is an absurd distortion. But forget the clock, and look at what is relevant: the number of increments of experience that make up our subjective times. Joanna, in her time scale, has been *as patient*, i.e., has sat through as many boring stretches of her life, in four minutes as I have in my wait through fifteen. I have been expecting her to be four times as patient as I am, and felt it a moral shortcoming, in need of discipline, when she does not measure up to this extraordinary expectation. We tend to excuse young daughters and be kind to them, but also to describe them as deficient in our own excellence. We retain the impatience, but begin to discontinue the kindness and excuses, when our sons of college age show incredible lack of prudence in planning ahead. Ten years from now, just two more years of study could make the difference between a well-paid, effective career and a precarious vagabondage, we explain. Measured by our own time sense, two years has been one twenty-fifth of my lifetime; not very long. For an

eighteen-year-old it is more than ten percent of his whole life
to date. If I were asked to commit five years of my career now
toward the prospect of security I do not now want, in the year
1991, it would not be my immediate impulse to embrace the
chance! I am not sure, either, that I would react kindly to the
insistence of my elders that the advantage was so obvious that
I was a fool and an ingrate for not seeing it, or taking their word
for it. Young men will judge the lengths of time by projecting
fractions of the total life-experience they have had, and the average content per calendar year of that experience, into anticipated plans; old men will do the same. Since it is the same
clock and calendar, we are tempted to assume that there is an
objective "length" to two years, the same for everyone. But what
we are doing is to substitute an irrelevant for a relevant type of
time, under the hypnotic delusion that equal time increments
must correlate with equal intervals of space.

This may sound less like a discussion of reality than a plati-
tudinous admonition for kindness to children. But it is in fact
a direct application of a metaphysical principle: that there are
multiple series of one-directional modal transformations each
of which is a time-series, and that contrary to general opinion,
increments that are *equal* in one time-line may well be *unequal*
when projected into another. To take scales which correlate
successive temporal increments of transformation with equally
extended spatial increments certainly makes the time-series so
defined more publicly useful; it has nothing to do with the
question of whether this peculiar type of time scale is in any
way exclusively *real*.

One of the most amazing things about subjective time is the
extent to which we ourselves structure and control it. We are
able, for example, to divide and order our experiences, memories, and anticipations quite unrealistically. Just as an observer
projects visual forms into an indeterminate field, we project
patterns of closure, separation, and differentiation onto our temporal adventures. In extreme cases, this results in monochrome
subjective time senses. Catatonia and mania are extreme examples of an inability to combine objective input of experience
with coherent subjective forms of time. Napoleon, a good ob-

server if not a great metaphysician, had a relevant remark. "Some men," he said, "always picture the future in their minds as a detailed, complete tableau. Such men are dangerous." I suppose he meant dangerous as field commanders; as human beings in private life, I think they are less dangerous than sad. What they are doing is confusing the closed detail of memory with anticipation: the future always fails, in some detail, to match the tableau that was expected. The sense of time is jammed in such a way that it can use only the perfective patterns which organize a past, even when it is the inceptive ones leading into a future that are objectively appropriate. Or we can find cases of refusal to accept time altogether; of inability to escape a knife-edge present to relate it to the rest of our life; of optimistic inceptive thinking which, perpetually hopeful, always begins afresh with no learning from experience that the future is not determined, but is indeed limited, by the past. (A poker player convinced on every hand that if he discards four cards, he will get four aces this time, is an extreme case in point.) Here is an area where metaphysics touches on psychology. We can offer some suggestions as to what does constitute a realistic modal patterning of time, and what selective attention to aspects of that pattern are responsible for wrong generalizations under emotional impulses toward security, self-assertion, self-annihilation, and flight. I should like to develop this theme with reference to language, and argue that the dominance of the past-pessimistic, perfective aspect over the future-euphoric, inceptive shows that the givers of names in Indo-European tongues have always been the old men of the tribe. I forbear both for lack of time and from a distaste for perpetrating any further discussions of language: a moratorium of half a century on this theme might do us good.[35]

Finally, let me point out a relation of applied metaphysics to longevity. We have so much control over time in our experience that we are able to regulate how many increments of subjective experience we encounter for a given unit of the time of calendar, clock, and life-span. Within certain objective limitations (which can be indicated, I think, by equations that are, like logical tables, very dull to read), the choice is our own. "Longevity" can be defined, of course, in two ways: in the extension of conscious experience through the extension sequence of calendar and clock; or in the total content of such experience in its sequence, intensity, and order. Each is a legitimate definition for its own purposes; since my present purpose is humanistic rather than actuarial, it is the second meaning that I have in mind. To illustrate my point, I would like to introduce a simple account of two of my own every-day adventures. Often—though not as often as I should—I go from my office in Saybrook College to the Yale Library.

On Monday, I am in a hurry to get there; a new book has just come in. My trip from office to library is an uninterrupted, single experience, taking about four minutes of wristwatch time. On Tuesday, I set out again, with less determination to hurry and get there. It is a late summer day, with a rising wind that feels as though autumn is near. I look up at the weather vane in the shape of a plump owl, who ornaments a campus tower. A grey squirrel scuttles past, running furiously along the Trumbull College wall. The wind shifts and now gusts blow across High Street from the Cross Campus; I look at the weather vane again, and see him turning majestically. That trip involved four increments of experience, and also took four minutes of wristwatch time. In other words, on Tuesday my excursion contained four times as many increments of experience per unit of clock time as it did on Monday! This is what I mean by creating more time for ourselves.

I hope these applications have been reasonable and clear. I have no doubt they have been interesting, since I agree with Kant that metaphysicians take a natural interest in God, freedom, and longevity (a surrogate here for immortality); and in this matter, every human being is a metaphysician by nature. The question in not whether we shall apply metaphysics, but whether we apply it well or badly.

An Appendix on Logic and Passage

My main thesis is that time is, of course, unreal; what Platonist can deny that? But different orders have different admixtures of non-being: all preserve some semblance of the pure order of number series and repeating cycle, but as we move from being to becoming the coerciveness and determinateness of this vestigial form decrease. I want here to illustrate a method of *proximate abstraction*, by isolation of relevant form without reduction of it to so much simpler a level that one loses the very peculiarities under study. I will take up three topics: the logical relations of a formal system with three "tenses" stated in its most general form; the alternative logical possibilities for "rules of passage" that can correlate changes of modality with some standard clock-and-calendar scale; and, briefly, the single formal objective limitation I can find that determines how we can structure, expand, or contract our subjective "experience time." In the first part, the interest lies in the generality of the logical relations: without more special information than we get from knowing that propositions have future possibilities as referents, there is incorrigible ambiguity in what we can determine about their logical relations. *However*, four distinct formal systems without this ambiguity result when we add additional postulates about the structure of the relevant realm of possibility. In the second part, a formal matrix is offered in partial explication of what seems the fact that truth-values of different types of statement change historically in different ways. I will not claim that this clears up the "logical peculiarities" of, for example, religious language, nor even that it offers an exhaustive plan of ways in which different kinds of talk are logically peculiar. But I will claim that it helps to clarify the question.[36] In the third section, I will suggest that human life faces us with constant choices between confused longevity and shorter-lived order. I will also offer one equation that is of considerable interest in defining, creating, or avoiding environmental *monotony*.

Suppose we use a four-valued logic, where 1 and 0 refer to *definite* truth or falsity, $\neq 0$ to an indefinite state of "non-falsity," $\neq 1$ to an indefinite state of "non-truth." I take $\neq 1$ to be the non-definite relation holding between a proposition with a future referent and the status of that referent as a possibility; $\neq 0$ is the special case in which the future referent is an *option*, i.e., where it is "actually" possible, and realizable by an increment of choice. (This was the suggestion I used in my article, "Logic and Time," *The Review of Metaphysics*[1965]. But my present scheme differs from and is much better than the one proposed in that article.) Using a "weak" notion of negation (so that $\sim \sim p = p$) and other standard connectives, the following table shows the resulting logic.

As I noted above, an article of Donald Sherburne's on Whitehead's treatment of "propositions" suggests a plausible interpretation for the fractional values of my tables.[37] A proposition is to be thought of as the relation between an actual occasion, its subjects, and possible forms, eternal objects or predicates, which that subject does or does not prehend. In cases where an asserted S-P relation matches the objective one, the propositions are called "conformal"; those where there is no such match are called "non-conformal." Of the two, Whitehead thought the non-conformal statements were even more important and interesting than the conformal ones. This follows from Whitehead's more general claim that intelligence arises as present facts suggest future alternatives which are hypothetical.[38]

But clearly there is a third class of propositions between the *simply true* conformal ones and the *simply untrue* non-conformal group. This is the set of *partially conformal* assertions. The S-P relation asserted is not impossible, but not wholly factual. There are varying degrees of what we may call hardening into factuality. When the correspondence of proposed alternatives and present fact is close, we have a high "partial conformality" value; a low one where it is not. These can now be treated as the fractional values of a logical calculus that is extended to include probabilities as well as 1 and 0 values. Professor John Cobb has some new insights into the role of such an analysis of propositions in their relation to inquiry and communication. When these are developed, as I hope they will be, they promise to support the usefulness of my systematic tables.[39]

Note that in this table, ' $\supset$ ' behaves much as we want "causal relevance" to behave: a future definitely implies the actual past, but "forward" inferences across tense lines are not definite. ("Causal relevance" here is limited to "efficient causality.") Also note that four compound values are '*': neither specifiable as

Table 5.1.   Logic with Two Indefinite Values: the Most General Case

		(1)	(2)		(3)	(4)	(5)
p	*q*	~*p*	*p*	*q*	*p*·(*p* *q*)	[*p*·(*p* ⊃ *q*)] ⊃ *q*	~*p* v *q*
1	1	≠1	1		1	1	1
1	0	≠1	0		0	1	≠1
0	1	≠0	1		0	1	1
0	0	≠0	1		0	1	≠0
1	≠1	≠1	≠1		≠1	*	≠1
0	≠1	≠0	1		0	1	≠0
≠1	1	1	1		≠1	1	1
≠1	0	1	*		*	*	1
≠1	≠1	1	*		*	*	1
1	≠0	≠1	≠0		≠0	≠0	≠0
0	≠0	≠0	1		0	1	≠0
≠1	≠0	1	≠0		≠1	≠0	1
≠0	1	0	1		≠0	1	1
≠0	0	0	0		0	1	0
≠0	≠1	0	≠1		≠1	*	≠1
≠0	≠0	0	≠0		≠1	≠0	≠0

definite nor as indefinite. This is not corrigible in any general scheme which claims to apply to all types of futures, just insofar as they are future.

The fact that certain values can't be determined in the completely general formal system which is common to any set of metaphysical assumptions is not surprising. My '*' values should be read as *variables*, the values of which will depend on the more specific logical contexts, L1–L5. Thus '*p* ⊃ *q* = *', when *p* ≠ 0, *q* ≠ 1, abbreviates: *p* ⊃ *q* in L1 = 0; and *p*   *q* in L2 = ≠ 1; and *p* ⊃ *q* in L3 = *f*(*q* − *p*); and *p* ⊃ *q* in L4 = *dI*(*p* v *q*).

Third, note that this will not be an easy logic to work with: familiar equivalences, such as that of *p*   *q* and ~ *p* v *q* break down, as do other rules, e.g., ~ (*p*.~ *p*). But also note that no assumptions are introduced beyond that of a fact—option—possibility, or modality, so that the plan has the maximum possible generality consistent with its interpretation as a logic applicable to passage.

Four special added postulates result in four standard logical systems as special cases of this table, cases in which all or some of the annoying ambiguities of the '*' values are removed.

Special Case I. Assume that there are future facts, but we do not know them. Assume further that "logic" is concerned with what is the case, rather than with vagaries in our determination of this. Then the referents of propositions reduce back to 1 or 0, and we get the standard two-valued calculus which works perfectly for factual and atemporal domains.

Special Case II. Assume that all possibilities are actually possible. This leads to a new and interesting system which my former colleague, Professor Milton Fisk, explored. The assumption makes it possible to replace both my $\neq 0$ and $\neq 1$ values by the single indefinite value, u. Two sets of logical constants preserve the difference between types and directions of inference.

Special Case III. This accepts Professor Fisk's postulate that all possibilities are actual, and adds that they can be arranged in branched distinct sets of successive options.[40] (Moves in chess are a typical case which these assumptions fit.) At this point, the general case reduces to a version of standard probability calculus. In its simplest form, we let P be the "probability" of p, defined as the number of occurrences of p's in an option set over the total number of elements $p + p'$. If the set is not "immediate," i.e., if its initial condition itself depends on selections made among "previous" sets, we correct P. The result is a probability scheme in which the probabilities of compound propositions as wholes are a function of those of their components. Notice that in a situation where the future is in fact ordered in this way, the '*' values of the general case become determinate fractions.

Special Case IV. Assume that, although precise fractional probabilities cannot be assigned, it is possible to discriminate roughly between "wider" and "narrower" indefinate ranges. That

Table 5.2. Specialization of Table 1 by Assumptions equaling Indefinite Values, with "Probabilities"

		(1)	(2)	(3)
p	q	$\sim p$	$p \supset q$	$\sim p \vee q$
1	1	0	1	1
1	0	0	0	0
0	1	1	1	1
0	0	1	1	1
1	Q	0	Q	Q
0	Q	1	1	1
P	1	$1-P$	1	1
P	0	$1-P$	$1-P$	$1-P$
P	Q	$1-P$	$(1-P)+Q$	$(1-P)+Q$
1	Q	0	Q	Q
0	Q	1	1	1
P	Q	$1-P$	$(1-P)+Q$	$(1-P)+Q$
P	1	$1-P$	1	1
P	0	$1-P$	$1-P$	$1-P$
P	Q	$1-P$	$(1-P)+Q$	$(1-P)+Q$
P	Q	$1-P$	$(1-P)+Q$	$(1-P)+Q$

Note. As indicated, the possibility p ⊃ q is computed as -pvq, that is $(1-P)$ plus Q

is, instead of $\neq 0$, we might be able to say that p has a value $\neq 0$, and between 1 and 1/2. This may be the way to represent an Aristotelian logic which actually does something with the propositions of "indefinite quantity" that figure in the *De Interpretatione*, but disappear in later "Aristotelian" logic.[41] One can find some clues to these indefinite ranges in passages where Aristotle defines "many," "few," "most," and so on. How useful the extension is in reasoning can only be determined by trying it out.

However, while the table of "modalities" and the logical relations between them can be given various interpretations as relations of tenses or aspects at any given state, there is nothing in its pattern to indicate the fact that time does pass—i.e., that some values are invariant, but others are subject to change. It is just this combination of fixity and variability that characterizes the world of becoming; and we need to add a rule of "passage" to complete the "definiteness" table. But what is the rule? This turns out to be a surprisingly interesting question, because the minimum formal conditions necessary for serial "passage" are very permissive. Starting with the case of descriptive propositions, which we have been tacitly assuming as the propositions in our logical table, the rule is clear. A logic applies to passage when its values divide into "facts" which remain fixed and definite, and "options" or "possibilities" where values become definite after a certain number of increments of transformation of option into fact.

$$[V (p)t + \neq (1 \text{ v } 0)] \quad [V (p)t0 + ndt = (1 \text{ v } 0)]$$
$$[V (p)t0 = (1 \text{ v } 0)] \quad [V (p)t0 + ndt = (1 \text{ v } 0)]$$
$$V (p)t - = (1 \text{ v } 0)$$
$$V (p)t0 = (\neq 0)$$
$$V (p)t + = (\neq 1).$$

This is a tidy flow, in which choices transform options into facts, possibilities become actualized or excluded, $t0$ is an objective ontological "now," and ndt any set of increments of clock-and-calendar "time." But is there any formal need that modal change and normal physical time-direction be related in this way? Not at all; for the rule could be generalized and still prescribe a passage situation.

$$[V (s)t \neq 0 = (1 \text{ v } 0)] \text{ V } [V (s)t \pm ndt = (1 \text{ v } 0)]$$
$$[V (s)t0 = (\neq 1. \neq 0)] \quad [V (s) \pm ndt = (1 \text{ v } 0)]$$
$$[V (s)t0 = (1 \text{ v } 0)] \quad [V (s)t \pm ndt = (1 \text{ v } 0)].$$
$$[V (s)t0 = \neq 0 \text{ v } 0)] \quad [V (s) \pm ndt = (1 \text{ v } 0)].$$

In this formula, s is a variable ranging over "statements"; V is extended to "expressive truth" or similar properties as well as standard "truth-value"; and while modalities change for some cases, not for others, with the "increments of passage," ndt, nothing says in what direction the change occurs. What made me think of this possibility of alternative logical patterns of changing truth and passage was the comment by Dr. Robert Neville that perhaps religious expressions lost some of their absolute expressive truth whenever they became past. (He did not mean to say, I am sure, that past expressions of this type are inadequate *if we can* grasp and reassert them in the present; but that *as past* expressions, they could only be fractionally "true" in a given present. In that case, there are a number of definable truth-and-passage patterns possible relating the ways modality stays fixed and changes relative to a $t0$, $t+$, and $t-$ fixed by the "physical sequence" given in our first, more specific, rules of passage. The fixed and changing modalities could lie in any combination of our three t-domains, as the table shows.

Table 5.3. Possible Relations of Changing Modalities to a Standard Clock-time System. (1 in this table equals a definite or fixed modality, 0 a modality that transforms with increments added or subtracted.)

	$t-$	$t0$	$t+$
1)	1	1	1
2)	1	1	0
3)	1	0	1
4)	1	0	0
5)	0	1	1
6)	0	1	0
7)	0	0	1
8)	0	0	0

Rows 1 and 8 are not types of passage; row 1, because it rather describes factual or atemporal statements, row 8 because it describes *incorrigibly* unfixable ones (Russell's paradox, for example). Row 4 is the standard pattern where fixed values are in $t-$, changing ones in $t0$ and $t+$. Row 6 is the pattern Dr. Neville suggests, where definite values are always in a present, but change to indefinite as one moves to $t-$ or $t+$. Promises, contracts, and so on are statements that *may* have the peculiar value-shift behavior pattern of line 5; but they may not. The point is the very light hand placed on the reins of passing time by the eternal forms, which set invariant boundaries and laws to passage.

Moving to the most elusive series that still have form enough to qualify as passing times, I would like to conclude by saying a bit more about the weathervane owl. So far as the formal definitions go, *any* sequence of modal transformations that meets the passage rule above is a set of increments of a time, ndt. Our ordinary preference is for special sets which we can correlate with congruent bits of spatial extension; but the preference is ours, not nature's. Our experiences, for example, insofar as we remember them as single episodes bounded by events, form a subjective time. There are only two controls that I can see imposing form on this series from without. The first is that it agrees with physical and biological process its direction: that is, that we can only divide happenings from each other into increments of experience when there is some objective change in the rate of acceleration of our "input" or sensations and ideas.[42] But these two objective limitations are such faint shadows of strict formal order that they are consistent with all varieties of experience, attention, and memory. One can see at once that hypersensitivity will result in a blurred confusion of events, with no stable states of experience identified and divided by them; and that total anaesthesia leads to a single, uneventful state making up the sole increment of a subjective life time. Human beings have the surprising, and not always welcome, power of trading *vividness* for *order*. (Vividness is defined here as the number of successive states of experience in a life-span, order as their concentrated hierarchical integration.) One kind of "concentration," and the one we usually stress in education, shuts off "distractions" and gets order at the price of vividness. An alternative power of attention, which we must add to our educational scheme, notices the individual, the concrete, the ephemeral; this increases vividness. For optimum human "longevity" we should find the best balance of both: vivid chaos is longer, subjectively, but lucid pursuit of echeloned goals and principles is necessary if life is to have its full value.

Chapter 6
Decisions:
Value Changes and Tenses

I N THIS DISCUSSION I intend to explore the rules for right choice that follow if there are incommensurable orders of value and if we assume that a "right" choice conserves or increases value or involves infinitely less value loss than any other. The key to this discussion is Robert Hartman's formal model of value orders, which I believe offers the best resolution to a paradox that follows from two of our fundamental intuitions that underlie decision and evaluation.[1]

Ever since there has been discussion of choice, there has been an intuitive conviction that while some values are additively related, others cannot be. There is no cash price, no degree of comfort, that can persuade a Socrates to give up his pursuit of wisdom or a Beowulf his quest for glory and honor.

At the same time we do have to compare all sorts of values in making decisions; and a second intuitive conviction we hold is that "better than" is an asymmetrical, transitive relation analogous to "greater than"—though a Minoan merchant probably would not have formulated his intuitive notion in so abstract a way. This second notion suggests at once that the number series is a suitable formal model for rational comparison and that the alternatives are either such a calculus or a rejection of the relevance of thought to action. If *A* is better than *B*, we want to know how much better, better for how many people, and better for how long. And we feel intuitively that these questions make sense.

Now these two intuitive notions, within the formal resources of pre-nineteenth-century mathematics, set up an antinomy that is irreconcilable. For, if we assign numbers on a scale to *A* and *B*, a sufficient number of additions of *A* (reaching $A.B + A$) will constitute a value total greater than B.[2] If Beowulf—as is the case—values both valor and treasure, the dragon should be able to avoid combat by offering a large-enough treasure hoard as a bribe. Honor is indeed partly measured by gifts, rings, and well-wrought arms in *Beowulf*; but bribery by the dragon would go against Beowulf's character and wreck the epic.[3] A familiar illustration, closer to home than heroes and dragons, is the application of hedonic calculus to the Indians and Joe. The calculus rests on the assumption that the right thing to do is that which produces the greatest excess of increments of pleasure over displeasure, each moment for each person to count as $+1$ or -1. In that case, if the Indians really enjoy burning Joe alive, that is the right thing for them to do. Nor can we get out of this by a "weighting" which sets Joe's displeasure equal to $-n$ on our value scale. For in that case it is right to burn him as soon as the number of tribal celebrants is increased to $n+1$. The result is squarely counterintuitive: Joe's life and dignity are simply more valuable than an afternoon of entertainment, however large the house.

As is often the case in dealing with mathematical concepts and models, our intuition is *almost* but *not quite* right. (Compare our intuitive notions of "inside" and "outside" with the precise formulation of these concepts in topology.)[4] And Robert Hartman has seen that if we extend the notion of cardinal numbers to include *transfinite* numbers, the two notions—that values can be ordered and compared by an arithmetical model and that some values are nonadditively related—become compatible. He suggests that there are three value orders, standing in "greater than" relation, that can be represented as having cardinal numbers n, aleph-null, and aleph-one. That does the needed trick as far as the two intuitive notions we have cited go: we keep comparability but without reducibility between orders.[5]

This tension between intuitions is more than a mere abstract analyst's curiosity. Historically poets and playwrights have tended to resolve it by denying the second of the pair—the relevance of calculation to action, while merchants and social scientists resolve it (after vague murmurs about dimensions and standpoints) by calculi that operationally reject the first. Ordinarily, I suppose, not too much damage is done: for ordinarily we are engaged *either* with an impersonal citizen and economic man, *or* with an epic villain or hero; and the engagement is reflected in our picking the single right-order value scale. But a Leibnizian single plane of finite permutations of property-chains, called "possible worlds," can lead to disaster when it fails to provide for infinite positive and negative changes in value.[6]

What may prove to be Robert Hartman's greatest insight, one that any Platonist or Hegelian must approve, is his recognition that mathematical innovations in set theory over the past century offer new models for the formalization of value theory.

The purpose of my present discussion is to continue the program of formalization in this area. In particular, I want to discuss an extension of the new set-theoretical model that makes it possible to incorporate calculation rules for "trivial," one-level choices within the formal structure of stratified value theory.

Let us begin with the intuitively evident fact that when we are making choices, we can order alternatives on scales of preference, using an asymmetrical transitive relation of "better than." If we like, this can be specified in terms of some arbitrary element used as measure: thus "better than (economically)," "better than (hedonistically)," and so on. The beauty of this way of thinking is that we can take the series of natural numbers as the formal model for value decisions, correlating "better than" in the value series with "greater than (in respect to units of type k)" in the number sequence. And the operations of arithmetic can be transferred more or less intact to operations of value comparison.

Because we know how to work with numbers, this is a natural model; and for complex calculations, such as are usual in economics and politics, it is hard to think of another that would be practicable. Yet at the same time, both the identification of "greater than" with "better than" and the assumption that units are available as "measures" of values, may lead to mischief. Plato, in his *Statesman*, observed that there are two kinds of measure, descriptive and normative.[7] Descriptive measure sets up a series simply by reapplying the "successor of" or "incrementally greater than" relation. But in the arts, for example, where we are concerned with the "best" size for a table, the series is structured differently: the right size lies in the middle of two series of increasing deviations, one in the direction "too much," the other in that of "too little." And in *evaluation*, it is the *smallest* deviation number which is best. Plato, in another dialogue, shows the catastrophic cultural results of equating "bigger" with "better" by an Atlantean civilization which had fine technology but no philosophy.[8] We will keep this qualification in the background. I am reluctant to bring it into the foreground, since it is hard for me to see how to specify a maximum "right amount" in a form the administrator or social scientist can use.

The other problem with using the numbers as a model for ordered values is a more serious one. When this is done, the result is a single value scale, rather than stratified value orders. And since we are dealing with *increments* of some kind, the system is Archimedean. That is, the addition of a sufficient number of value increments to a given value will form a total that exceeds any larger term in the series. This, of course, is illustrated by the paradoxical result of applying strict hedonic calculus to the problem of the Indians and Joe. Since what ought to be done is, by definition in that calculus, what produces the greatest excess of units of pleasure over units of displeasure, if there are enough Indians who would enjoy burning Joe at the stake, this is what they ought to do. All sorts of variations on this theme offend our moral intuitions and our sensitivity to values, yet they are built into the Archimedean system of such a formal axiology.

Now, what Robert Hartman proposed was to extend the arithmetical formalism in the light of Cantor's work with set theory to include *transfinite* as well as *finite* cardinal numbers. By correlating value types or value orders with the "greater than" relation as it holds between transfinite cardinals, a formal axiology suited to "stratified" value theory is the result.[9] The reason is that "infinite" sets are not Archimedean: the addition of *any* number of elements will not make a "lesser" cardinal equal to or greater than a "larger" one. This follows from the peculiar property of transfinite cardinals that for some parts, the part is as great as the whole. And from that, if follows that "addition" and "subtraction" are not cardinally relevant operations: they don't change cardinality.[10] (Once more, Plato had a clear notion that some such "stratified" relation holds among value orders. Perhaps this is most naively and simply put in the *First Alcibiades*, a dialogue from the Academy, if not Plato's own. "What price would you take for your courage, Alcibiades?" Socrates asks. "No price whatever," he answers, "I would far rather die, Socrates, than become a coward." If wealth, then, is treated as a first order of value, say n, courage is of another order, aleph-sub-zero.)

In our particular universe, it seems that there are three primary levels of value. These are the orders of systemic, extrinsic, and intrinsic value recognized in Hartman's theory. The first of these has an order of complexity of relevant properties of cardinality N, the second aleph-null, the third of aleph-one (which we will take for our purposes to be the cardinal number of the continuum). There are operations of repeated evaluation which correspond to raising to a power in the arithmetic of transfinite numbers. Thus an object which out of context has a value N, may for me, because of its association with other values, be transvalued into N to the aleph-null power, raised to the next value order. Analogously, a value may be neutralized by transposition, be disvalued and as a result lead to an axiological product of a lower order (to accomplish this result, however, one needs to introduce an unorthodox operation into Cantor's set theory).

In a later part of this chapter, I will try to show how admirably this scheme detects and calculates value-order confusion. Whenever we choose to treat an individual as an abstract person, a person as a thing, a thing as a individual human being, the calculus shows at once that we are transposing orders, and thus making infinite mistakes in valuation.

But the non-Archimedean protection of stratified value types has an unhappy limitation. As the model stands, it admits only of repeated comparisons based on value *level*. In other words, only "valuations" involving degrees of infinity can be operated with, and "choices" which may be needed *within* any given level find no mathematical representation. I suspect that prior to Cantor, the confused character of the notion of "infinity" deterred theorists from building mathematical models of stratified value theory. And I also suspect that Hartman's first attempt to use notions of "infinity" is a pioneering venture that will require extension if philosophy and social science are to join forces.

One extension of the formal model seems to me to represent and accommodate both one-level and cross-level "better than" calculations. For, in addition to transfinite cardinals, there are transfinite ordinal numbers in modern set theory. Thus *omega* represents the position of the final term in the series of natural numbers. The cardinal number corresponding to this term is aleph-null, since there are a transfinite number of positions. And I gain nothing by writing, for example, k plus omega: this simply indicates that I pass position k on the way to position omega. On the other hand, the number omega plus k designates a position k units *beyond* the end of the omega series. Now, omega and omega plus k are both infinite sets of elements, hence both have the cardinal number aleph-null. *But* omega plus k is "greater than" omega alone in that the "plus k" component goes "beyond" the omega series. The result is that, if we represent values on aleph levels by *transfinite ordinals*, we get the best of both worlds. In respect to *value orders*, these numbers are *non-Archimedean*: repeated addition will never shift cardinal type. In respect, however, to the ordinal "greater than" relation, the plus k components *are* Archimedean, and are subject to our ordinary arithmetical operations of comparison: addition, subtraction, division, multiplication. We need three "level characteristics" to indicate cardinal order: thus, if a finite ordinal is 0, our three index components will be 0, omega, and omega* (omega raised to the omega power: the ordinal number of all series of ordinal numbers, which has a cardinal number of aleph-one). Our plus-*k* components can be chosen from any scale of increments—cost, pleasure, utility—correlated with the standard number series and assigned the number *n.k*. Within its level, the series of ordinals is now Archimedean, permitting choices that do not involve infinite differences between them.

Halmos (*Naive Set Theory*, pp. 33ff.) comments on the properties of transfinite ordinal numbers.[12] As most pure mathematicians are, he is a Platonist: it does not occur to him to talk in terms of *assigning* rules or properties; rather, he looks to see what the objective facts are, and comments on them as an observer. "Some of the properties of addition for ordinal numbers are good and some are bad," he writes. He counts as "good" the identities $a + 0 = a, 0 + a = a, a + 1 = 1^+$, and $a + (b + c) = (a + b) + c$. He continues, "Almost all the bad behavior of addition stems from the failure of the commutative law. Sample: $1 + \text{omega} = \text{omega}$, but . . . omega $+1 \neq$ omega." He finds a similar set of good and bad properties for multiplication (p. 34). Among good properties, he counts $a0 = 0 \ 0a = 0, a1 = 1, 1a = a, a, (bc) = (ab)c$, and $a(b + c) = ab = ac$. However, the commutative law for multiplication fails, and so do many of its consequences. For instance 2 omega $=$ omega, but omega 2 $\neq$ omega. ("Think of an infinite sequence of ordered pairs" as a case of the former, and "think of an ordered pair of infinite sequences" as a case of the latter.) For transfinite ordinal numbers, Halmos has already proven that $a + a = a$, and that if b is transfinite, $a + b = b$ whether a is finite or not. Also, $a \cdot a = a$, and $a \cdot b = b$ when b is transfinite. His final comment on "Ordinal Arithmetic" (p. 85) is that "Not all the familiar laws of exponent hold." For instance, $(ab)^c$ is in general different from $a^c b^c$. "Example: $(2.2)^{\text{omega}} = 4^{\text{omega}}$, but $(2^{\text{omega}} . 2)^{\text{omega}} = \text{omega }^2$.

Robert Hartman and I were both pleased to find that modern mathmetics could offer a formal model that combines the two types of "calculation." But we did not agree about some questions of interpretation. In his eagerness to protect the autonomy of axiology, I argued, he protected stratification, but at the expense of leaving no room for certain familiar choice situations. For example, in my world, there can be and often are "trivial choices": the alternatives lie at the same point on a single scale on a single level. Exceptionally, some value from a higher order may be relevant, but this, I hold, is the exception. In an earlier brief discussion of my "trivial choices" project, I took the example of myself choosing a lunchtime salad from the Saybrook College salad bar. ("Formal Value Theory: Transfinite Ordinal Numbers and Relatively Trivial Practical Choices," *Journal of Human Relations*[21] [Second Quarter 1973], 211–16.)[13] I will repeat it here, as a paradigm test case for discussion, because Robert Hartman addressed it in his reply to my *J.H.R.* note. (Robert S. Hartman, "Reply to Eckhardt and Brumbaugh," *J.H.R.* 21: 220–26.) I frequently eat lunch at Saybrook College, and pick up a salad from the selection offered by our salad bar. Ordinarily, it doesn't matter much to me, to the college, or to the universe, whether I choose pickled beets or cottage cheese. (One can find exceptions, when my choice has something to do with lower-order conditions essential to higher-order value. For example, if by taking nonunion lettuce I help to undercut a union strike, this is bad on the level of extrinsic value. Or if I, a Pythagorean, choose a salad of lima beans, this is bad on the level of intrinsic value. But it seems to me these cases are exceptional, and not the rule.)

The final result, if I am right, is a scheme that makes it possible to combine Robert Hartman's "stratified" orders of value and the useful nonstratified calculations of the various sorts of "value theory" more ordinarily found in economics and politicial science. In particular, I think this model provides for many types of value comparison, and I think that our actual behavior and actual problems require its flexibility in types of valuing and decision.

On the other hand, until someone with more mathematical ability than my own sharpens this formalism, and we test it against various cases, it is not a certainty that there will be a complete axiological consistency. At least one doesn't run into the Indians and Joe. But in certain kinds of universe, where there is no room for triviality, it may be impossible to combine stratified and nonstratified calculi without some contradiction. Still, I think I can establish a formal proof of the *possibility* of "trivial" decisions.

By various strategic devices of using the "greater than" relation between transfinite ordinals, then correlating the ordered set with ordinary measures, we can still use simple arithmetical formulae for value comparison on any given level. And this, too, is what we want if the model is to match the properties of our ordinary behavior in discussing and deciding value questions. For among *comparable* alternatives it takes no philosopher, but only information, prudence, and a computer to decide which is more accurate, or more efficient, or least deviant from a consensus of preferences. It does take philosophic insight to decide when, if ever, a high value on one order of scale compensates for a low value on another. Suppose, for example, that we find a way of teaching aesthetic sensitivity to grade-school students that is very interesting for them, but very inefficient because it is expensive and slow. We also have an efficient but deadly program which gets whatever counts as the "right" response to an objective appreciation test cheaply and quickly. The choice here is no longer a "horizontal" measure on a single scale, but involves a "cross-level" one that raises philosophic problems (though of course it also involves all sorts of "horizontal" evaluation).[14] Finally the issue may boil down to whether the value of aesthetic appreciation is measurable by the number of "right" responses on an objective test. The case is very similar here to the problem of tense or aspect in logical inference: usually it is irrelevant, but *if* we cross aspect lines, we need to answer some radical philosophic questions before we can avoid self-referential inconsistencies.[15]

Before going on, however, let me note another very basic ethical intuition: there are times when a single choice or act that does transpose value orders is, in its context, the best and the right one. This intuition involves the introduction of value changes through time, which we will return to presently.[16]

I also think Hartman is right in his use of a principle of plenitude—of ontological complexity—to discriminate his three orders of value. If, as he holds, value is the adequacy of a thing to
the appropriate concept, there are indeed three kinds of adequacy and three kinds of appropriateness that are important to
distinguish. (There may well be more; I can see a good case for
at least five orders rather than three.)

The first case to consider is the match between a thing and
the *definition* of its concept. Such a criterion—a definition—
isolates a minimal set of essential properties, so that if any is
lacking, the concept does not apply. *Systemic value*, the match
between definition and case at hand, is always 1 or 0; either this
plane figure *is* a triangle or it *is not*. If I erase one of the sides,
I have not turned a "better" triangle into a "worse" one, but
have turned a triangle into a non-triangle—and I must find a
different defining concept to evaluate what this non-triangle
now is. This systemic value has the sort of simplicity and ex-
haustibility that can be represented by finite integers; its order
of plenitude is n or k; its parts are tightly conjoined, admitting
no omission or variation.

The second case is the match between a thing and the *exposition* of its concept, Hartman's *extrinsic value*. The exposition
adds on to the definition of a concept a set of properties which
are further specification: these are *not* logically necessary, but
are necessary in the sense that an instance must have all (or
some) of them in addition to the minimal defining set. If we
were to identify the definition with an *essence* or *form*, the
exposition would become a *type* or *type specimen*. It seems to
me that insufficient attention is given by Hartman to the difference between *form* and *type*. The type is not a minimum but a
maximum set: its properties are more specific in the alternatives
they exclude, where the form is far more open and permissive;
the type admits of degrees of approximation and keeps its relevance as criterion in the face of omission or transposition of
specific characteristics. In fact, Hartman's scheme of extrinsic
evaluation resurrects an Aristotelian logic with propositions of
"indefinite quantity" to describe degrees of type realization.[17]

The instances are "better" as they approach the maximum presented in the exposition.

The most relevant example for an ethical discussion is that of the relation of X as a *human being* to X as a *person* in a social-legal scheme. But the logical relations stand out more clearly if we begin again with the triangle. "A closed plane figure bounded by three straight lines" defines the concept we are applying, but tells us nothing about the respective lengths of side, size of angle, or surface color. But from each of these sets of properties—side length, angle size, and color—the instance must have just one definite set, which excludes all the other alternatives of this quantitative or qualitative spectrum. And not all combinations from different sets are compatible: obviously side lengths and angle sizes codetermine each other. These alternative possibilities for schematization taken together are an exposition of the concept. The logical relations are of three types: (1) The *defining* properties must all necessarily apply; a schema that destroyed any of them would also destroy the identity of the type as triangle. (2) Of the alternative sets of shapes, sizes, etc. *some* item of the set must apply *if* we are to have an existent triangle, not just the pure concept of triangularity. (3) Within each set the presence of any one specifying property *excludes* the others; and between sets it may exclude some others (angle size and side length do stand in this relation; angle size and surface color do not). This schematic triangle is an entity halfway between the realms of systemic and of extrinsic value: it has greater complexity than the pure definition, but in the absence of a context indicating some function, we cannot set up a maximum-to-minimum ordering of the added specifying set of properties.

A legal "person" offers a case of a type which does permit maximum-to-minimum evaluative ordering. A human being is essentially defined, let us say, by freedom, reason, sensitivity, and creativity. But these do not yet tell us what someone's role, rights, and relations to others are in a schematized society, where his or her status is specified by custom and law. The best society will then have the maximum properties of individual realization of full humanity, and this is greater when all human beings are recognized as legally equal than when they are not.

The person, as opposed to the essence, obviously has an infinitely greater complexity: an adequate description would require an infinite enumeration of compossible properties. This requirement is particularly clear if we consider the various deviations, the partial realizations of the perfect type, and alternative subtypes through which the pure type may be realized, and so on. There is obviously a sense in which history can combine in one system rules and insights that are ethically inconsistent or even ontologically mistaken.[18]

The peculiar problems of types and expositions of concepts need much exploration. For ethics, though, we can be satisfied with the distinction between a human being (systemic value) and a person (extrinsic value), and the observation that the latter is infinitely more complex than the former.

On the level of intrinsic value we come to the individual. He or she adds his or her own style, interpretation, unique space-time adventures and constructions to the more abstract identity of a self as a person in society; and this continuum of individual adventure is once again infinitely more complex than the person or the type. If we indicate the degree of plenitude of the *systemic* norm as *n* and of the *extrinsic* as aleph-null, the degree of *intrinsic* value becomes aleph-one.

The history of axiology seems to involve an opposition between emphasis on the principle of plenitude and emphasis on the principle of limitation. On the one hand, Hartman suggests that "better than" is equivalent to "ontologically more complex than"; some very interesting results can be calculated directly from the "greater than" relationship in his model. On the other hand, the Platonic tradition has equated "better than" with "more essential than," so that the forms, on the level of systemic value, are more real than their instances and so "better." After at least one reading of the *Republic* we would get the following result: the form is no better if it has instances than if it has not; the instance has no identity, hence no value, if it is not an instance of the form. But the system of the cosmos is better if forms are instantiated: this is an axiological, not strictly an ontological, judgment. Or, to the degree that it is an ontological judgment, it rests on the power of the good to establish cross-level relevance among instances, types, and forms.[19]

The Platonist's point may be introduced into our formal model in the following way. If A is a necessary condition for B, then the value of A is equal to the value of B. This is the principle of limitation. It works differently for the relation of instances to definition and of instances to explication. If to be an authentic individual is impossible without conserving the defining properties of a human being, respect for individuality cannot be greater than respect for humanity. But even though to be an individual requires a human community where one is a person in *a* context of order and law, the principle does not require us to value every detail of the current system as though this were the *only* type of organization that could provide law and order. In fact, combined respect for consistency and law may dictate revising or even rejecting some folkways and subordinate statutes in the interest of a better society.[20]

It is here that the difference between a definition and an explication, between a form and a type, becomes crucial to legal and political discussion. The temptation is to identify the current organization with a *definition* of what it is to be human and to equate every detail of that system with the value of full individuality, or to reject the system as a whole because some properties are inconsistent with such individuality.

If we can establish the limitation relation in such a way that to be an individual necessarily presupposes being essentially a human being and also presupposes being a person in *some* type of social community though not in any one unique type, it turns out that Hartman's distinction of value orders by plenitude and the Platonic insistence on orders of limitation are capable of being combined consistently in the model of value types we are trying to set up.

Perhaps we can return now to ethics and to the results that follow from the rule for choice that "a choice ought not to result in an infinite decrease in value." Or, put the other way, "a choice should always conserve or increase value." On any given value scale, as we have said, the question of selecting a larger value is a matter of experience, skill, and prudence; no properly ethical issues are likely to arise. But when a choice reverses the real structure of value orders, the transposition represents an infinite decrease in value over at least a one-choice increment of time. A morally bad choice thus always involves a mistake in its logic or in its motivation. Through ignorance one may incorrectly *believe* that value orders are not involved as in reality they are; through vice one may *will* that value orders not be related as they are. A third factor here is insensitivity—not *perceiving* that orders are related as they are or not *appreciating* their relation. Ordinarily we test the axiological correctness of choices by projecting their consequences: if my decision were repeated, magnified, observed as a rule, what would the consequent, long-range value change with time be? If it would be a transposition of orders, or a reduction to zero, it is in itself bad—not just because of its consequences, but because of its intrinsic contradiction of the axiological order. I think a case can be made for the fact that all types of ethical theory agree on some use of a "consequences over the long run" test as relevant to right choice. They differ in regard to whether unfavorable, long-run consequences show a logical, prudential, or aesthetic defect in the motives of that choice itself.[21] They agree in assuming that choices should increase or at least conserve value through passing time.

It seems to me that three rules, derivable from the model of orders of value, offer axioms for an ethical calculus. Two and one-half of the three sound like Kant; but the final half of the final rule is non-Kantian.[22]

Rule 1. A Choice Must Be Realizable. Not only are there things that cannot be chosen, but they ought not to be chosen. Sheer logical or physical impossibilities are not alternatives with positive value. Perhaps the most interesting case here would be the desire to make x a better F by destroying it as an F altogether. It is not possible to make people better human beings by taking away their freedom and imposing all decisions from external coercion. It is not possible to alter the past. It is not possible for me to jump over the Empire State Building. And so on. But, as my first example shows, logical and temporal entailments are different things. That first example is, of course, logically impossible; but it is temporally possible in the sense that, in the expectation that the consequent will follow, I can indeed affirm and create the antecedent. Unhappily, given time, the pattern "first, *A*, with the expectation that *A* implies *B*; then non-*B*" is a genuine historical possibility. So the first rule is weaker than a Kantian would want it; things that are simultaneously, not successively, inconsistent with logic, physics, and ethics are excluded. This might, of course, be taken as a *definition* of choice, not as a *rule*. But it follows as a theorem from our calculus: an impossibility has a value of 0, hence, it is less than any nonzero alternative.

Rule 2. A Choice Must Be Repeatable in Space and Time without Infinite Decrease in Value. This rule may amount to saying that if there is an atemporal, logical inconsistency between means and ends, there will also be a temporal incompatibility over a sufficient span of time. The reason for this rule is the normal human shortsightedness that forgets the hierarchy of scales of value. When *X* on *S*1 is greater than *Y* on *S*1, the counsel of expediency is to choose *X*. If it turns out that repetition of *X* leads to a disaster even on *S*1, the reason may be that we forgot to look at another value scale of a different order, *S*. There is very little deterioration of the environment, and very much financial gain, in disposing of the waste from a paper mill in the Androscoggin River. But there is a reversal of the values of human survival and large dividends involved in the choice, a transposition that shows very clearly under the test of consequences that magnify the transposition involved. More often, probably, the result is not that repetition of *X* ever leads to a disaster on the *S*1 scale itself, but that it does reduce value infinitely on the *S* scale. This rule implies a definition of justice, of a person, and of immortality. In the calculus we are using, a value transposition may be either one in which we put systemic value ahead of intrinsic, extrinsic value ahead of nonarbitrary systemic, extrinsic value ahead of the entire class of possible intrinsic value, intrinsic value that contradicts all extrinsic value ahead of extrinsic value (logically impossible, but not so temporally; this point holds for the other cases, too), and so on.

Rule 3. On the Level of Intrinsic Value Every Choice Should Be Repeatable without Infinite Loss of Value, but No Choice Should Be Repeated. The necessary condition of individuality is instantiation of a type: a human being with no status, context of rules, or society could not also have individuality. But the converse is also true: an individual has the unfortunate power to choose to be merely a person—predictable, repetitive, entirely typical. There are certainly justifications for this choice: it may be much more comfortable, and we certainly cannot argue that it is unjust or antisocial or inefficient. But to give up authenticity and creativity is to make a choice that does lead to putting value of order aleph-null ahead of order aleph-one.[23] Aesthetic interest diminishes with literal repetition: *literal* here means, not the same in general outline, for that is inevitable and all right, but the same in full, concrete texture, interpretation, and detail. Value of order aleph-one depends on novelty, idiosyncrasy, and adventure; the universe would be the worse without it. True, limitation is its essential condition; but we need plenitude within the boundaries of limitation. If the long-range implications of automation, or teaching machines, or public schools are to destroy and negate the right to style, we had better revise them before we choose to endorse them. The revision takes the form, of course, of a reconstructed type which leaves open the range of aleph-one value. This is the addition to Kant: for a being with aesthetic sensitivity it would be an aesthetic contradiction to choose the dull over the interesting, the painful over the pleasant.[24] Our law of contradiction therefore operates on the level of interests, as well as that of reason and that of will; I would contradict my identity as a human being by acting to reinforce anesthetized dullness.[25]

Formalization has several virtues, not least among them that it provides a way for carrying out Descartes's fourth rule of method, to conduct exhaustive reviews and enumerations.[26] Those activities, in turn, challenge our imagination to invent and consider cases, to find images, myths, and problems that we might well not have thought of in the normal, well-ordered chains of ideas that Descartes's third step of method recommends. So, given the indications we have had of the purpose, limits, and ambiguities of the formalizations of value orders, it may be interesting simply to set out the possibilities of value change from past through present into future, using Hartman's abbreviations, *I, E, S,* in a Table of Calculations. The table does not take account of 0 values, nor does it take account of "essential" *S* values; i.e., cases where *S* as a necessary condition must be set equal to *E* or *I*. The result is that the needed Platonic qualifications of Hartman's theory are not adequately represented in the table.

Rows 1, 14, and 27 of the table are simple cases in which value is conserved: an entity preserves or recovers its identity through passage. This fact implies a certain novelty in respect to choices and adventures for row 27, since mere endurance or subsistence (rows 1 and 14) will lead to a loss of intrinsic value. Rows 10 and 19 are bad by any standard; they involve the respective choices to reduce persons to things or to reduce individuals to things. These negative choices point up the need for calculations of *value orders*, which caution us against them. Let *S* be material efficiency, or abstract ideology, or profit; if the higher reading of the course chosen on the relevant *S* scale has not been balanced against the consequences on the *E* and *I* scales, the result is a permanent value loss. Lines 13 and 25 show a similar pattern, except that the value change is a future consequence, not an immediate concomitant, of the decision. (But it is a consequence of the value criteria by which the decision was made; *consequence* here is a stronger relation than mere historical succession.) Lines 2 and 5 are desirable patterns, in which work with ideas or materials is made relevant to better functioning of the society. (New work with computers in the interest of eventual better information for representative governments would be a case in point here.)[27] Lines 9 and 18 represent new aesthetic insights and interpretations that add value to systemic or extrinsic situations. These insights and interpretations are also desirable. Lines 3 and 12 have the same pattern. Line 6 is the pattern Whitehead had in mind for "social progress," which was to lead to "depth of individuality."[28] Line 15 is a similar pattern of progress, except that here we are readjusting extrinsic rather than systemic values.

We are left with two types of pattern: failures and temporary corrections. Surgery, therapy, and enforced rehabilitation fall under the second of these kinds. Medical treatment may involve the temporary handling of an individual simply as a complex mechanism, a thing. In itself, then, it is bad; but we decide it is good when the only open choices are the *I S S* or the *I S I* pattern. Law in its corrective role, again, is good when the *only* alternatives are I E I, I E E, I E S, I S S. But obviously this situation

Table 6.1. Calculations

#	t–	t0	t +	Vc/t
1	S	S	S	0
2	S	S	E	
3	S	S	I	+
4	S	E	–	
		S		
5	S	E	E	+
6	S	E	I	+
7	S	I	S	–
8	S	I	E	–
9	S	I	I	+
10	E	S	–	
	S			
11	E	S	E	–
12	E	S	I	+
13	E	E	S	–
14	E	E	E	
15	E	E	I	+
16	E	I	S	–
17	E	I	E	–
18	E	I	I	+

Table 6.1. Calculations

#	t–	t0	t +	Vc/t
19	I	S	S	–
20	I	S	E	–
21	I	S	I	–
22	I	E	S	–
23	I	E	E	–
24	I	E	I	–
25	I	I	S	–
26	I	I	E	–
27	I	I	I	0

is much more complex than the case of medicine, and our natural temptation to identify the two is a way of evading this complexity.[29] (Line 11 represents another medical alternative, I think, where we can restore effective social and vocational functioning without involving individuality and authenticity positively or negatively.) There is a tempting similarity between correction and education: to treat the individual pupil as a thing to be processed or an anonymous "student" to be informed. But, of course, there are infinitely better patterns open here, such as *S E I, E E I, E I I, I I I,* and even *S E E.* (The scheme is complicated because for certain technical purposes—such as curriculum design—we need to think of human potentialities as developing successively into actual characteristics. Thus, nursery-school students need things to play with, and they need gradual socialization leading to group activities proper to kindergarten levels. Empirical studies, though, are beginning to show the extent of value loss when parents and teachers ignore the fact that the *I I I* pattern is both the best and the most realistic criterion for educational design.)[30]

The analogy with medicine and law suggests that a corrective value pattern may sometimes justify political revolution. But the pure corrective value patterns represent conservation, not progress; and they represent infinitely less desirable alternatives if any of the "progress" value patterns are open. Current political discussion mirrors current discussion of value theory in general, as well as in other specific situations: an antinomy between the principles of plenitude and those of limitation.

The remaining patterns are cases of failure. Failure—pure failure that crosses value orders—is bad. It always involves some mistake about the consequence or the relative importance of the present moment. It can be eliminated by education: education in logic, physics, ethics, and aesthetics. And there is an infinite gain in this elimination when patterns of progress replace patterns of failure.

In working with his model, Robert Hartman introduces operations to indicate the way in which values of different order are themselves valued.[31] I have taken a different direction, trying to see what happens if they are descriptively compared, assuming that at least sometimes their objective types can be determined and agreed upon.[32]

The Sunday *New York Times* is full of case studies and editorial remarks that show the current importance of cross-type value comparison. Should federal aid be given to parochial schools? Should it be given to the individual children who are pupils in the schools? If so, should it be limited to expenses for their health and safety, not for other phases of their education? Should colleges give students more of a role in policy-making? Should state legislators pass bills making correction mandatory for draft protestors? Should we withdraw slowly, quickly, or not at all from our military and political commitments abroad? Is *poverty* a state of affairs, a state of mind, or both; and how is it to be corrected? Or is *correction* the right word?

All of these questions are so vivid and so engaging that in our present concerns we are apt to overlook the dry abstraction of such a matrix as the formal parade of *I*, *S*, and *E* above. But when it is overlooked, value change with time is likely to be a spectacular case of failure rather than a progress pattern.

Chapter 7
Metaphysical Systems:
And the Study of Time

L ET ME BEGIN by telling a fable. Suppose that there is a planet near Tau Ceti with people on it. But it has a homogeneous surface, and its inhabitants are very much alike genetically and culturally. For centuries, scientists there have been trying to decide what the nature of our earth is, on the basis of reports from rocket probes sent to different latitudes and longitudes. Each laboratory gets an interpretable result, but different from the others. For example, the scientists at *A* find the reports suggest an earth which is fluid, with a surface temperature above freezing; but the data recorded at *B* suggests an earth of solid rock, so cold that it must be covered with ice. Over the years, each laboratory has repeated its observations; re-calibrated its instruments; and accused the other group of errors in observation. Finally, a Conference is held, and three suggestions are offered. The first suggestion is that the differences are simply a matter of language: it is a question about the way we should use the phrase "surface of the earth." The meaning will be established once we all know how the phrase is used. A second suggestion is that the problem is not simply linguistic, but conceptual. We are constructing alternative models to match our observations: the data themselves are ambiguous enough to fit any of the competing conceptual schemes. And no observation will be able to confirm or disconfirm them.

The third suggestion—and in this imagined case the correct one—is that the difficulty is in a sense metaphysical. Living on a planet with surface uniformity, we neighbors of Tau Ceti assume that reality, wherever we observe it, will have surfaces that are uniform. But *in fact* "the" surface of the earth may well be differentiated into zones of hot and cold, of moist and dry, of earth and fire.

My present chapter assumes that past philosophical and literary discussions of time present the same conflicting reports as my hypothetical earth-probing rockets. And I propose to explore the possibility that the reason for the differences in reports is due to differences in the structures of the regions of time itself. I do not deny that our patterns of language and our conceptual paradigms select and emphasize different properties, but I do claim that all of the properties so selected are in some way objectively there. There is no more point in repeating past observation and argument in this case than there would have been, in my earth-probe example, in repeatedly sending rockets to the same latitude and longitude already explored by each laboratory.

In our discussions of time, whether everyday or technical, there is one metaphysical presupposition hidden which is plausible but mistaken. This is the assumption that time is enough like an abstract class or like a concrete physical object so that the law of identity will apply to it in the same way it does to substances and abstractions. If this is so, then it follows that as between contradictory properties, time can have only one of the pair, to the exclusion of the other. For example, if inspection and experiment indicate that time is continuous, we jump to the consequence that time cannot be discrete, since if continuity is represented by P, discreteness is non-P.

Historically, when there have been alternative exclusive accounts of time, we have inspected them with a view to selecting the right one, and rejecting the rest. This is perhaps clearest on a naive pragmatic level, where both machinist and artist tend to take the relevant properties of time with which they work, and to generalize these into a proposed account of the sole real nature of temporality. The two generalizations are radically different in respect of time's continuity or discreteness, its causal single-line determinism or branching option trees, its reversibility, the kind of logic that best applies to it, and so on. If time is a kind of thing that only one such definition can apply to, the study of time reveals a situation that is absurd.

I propose to show that there have in fact been four alternative accounts of time's reality on each of three levels of formality. Each of the four, on each level, is plausible and coherent; no two, on any level, are mutually consistent if consistency entails a strict law of identity. My three levels could be described as time considered purely qualitatively, as it is in myth and literature, on the most concrete step. Next, a second level considers time relationally, as it appears in a pragmatic world of substances, causes, and techniques. Third, we move to the more abstract consideration of time from the aspect of quantity: the mathematical and logical structures that offer formal models for time. Kantians will note that I have not mentioned modality; it is possible that the antinomies of my three levels can be resolved if we find a way to apply that fourth category. But my own generation of these levels is Platonic: I take them to match the three lowest segments of Plato's "Divided Line" in *Republic* 6–7.[1]

Let me begin with the level of abstract systems: of logics, philosophies, and mathematical models. Here, historically, there have been four families of philosophic systems in the West, all consistent and useful, but differing in what each presupposes to be the correct *direction* and the correct *method* of philosophic explanation. I will not argue just now that there must be only these four; but I will say that the fourfold classication has a surprisingly wide currency, and that no fifth coordinate system family has ever made a place for itself in the competition.

A formal system, I have said, will be defined in terms of what it assumes to be correct philosophic explanation. As to explanatory *direction*, one may postulate either a move toward the formal or toward the physical. We may, that is, look for the realities of things by seeking abstract types, structures, species, natures; or by seeking physical elements, natural processes, media, causal linkages. The formalist will emphasize logical causality, the physicalist physical. Both Platonism and Aristotelianism are classical philosophies with commitments of a formalist type; atomism and modern process philosophy both fall into the class of systems using a physical explanatory direction. For *method* of explanation, there are also two possible preferences, *analytic* and *synthetic*. An analytic explanatory method tries to underscore the differences between things, to move toward separate elements, or particles, or species, or specimens. The synthetic method, on the other hand, stresses continuities and similarities: it seeks description in terms of continuous, total fields—of logical space, or physical, or aesthetic, or whatever. The four combinations of preferred direction and method define the four families of Western philosophic system.[2]

Perhaps the way in which a system is defined by its assumed notion of explanation is seen most clearly in the case of the atomic theories. These are systems that combine physical direction with analytic method. The result is that an atomist seeks indivisible, distinct elementary parts in his search for reality. (Those parts may, of course, be physical or psychological or linguistic "atoms.") Explanation combines the analysis into elements with a construction of complexes and causal chains by contact and transfer of momentum. (Which we must take metaphorically in the psychological and linguistic dimensions.) Democritus, Epicurus, Hume, and Russell at one stage, all fall into this family.

Opposed to atomism both in direction and method is the family of Platonism. Platonic systems are committed to a formal direction and a synthetic method of explanation. The attempt is to grasp a timeless form—a determinate defining pattern in an abstract field of logical space. But in that field, each form is defined by its relation to the other structural parts and to the whole. The general pattern is one of formal hierarchy. Explanation then must order formal parts hierarchically, indicate a relevant vertex, and study the participation by which structures ingress into and determine history and fantasy.

Aristotelianism represents a third system type, designed by Aristotle to mediate between Platonism and atomism, and sharing something with each. The Aristotelian systems have a formal explanatory direction, but an analytic method of explanation. Thus where a Platonist has logical hierarchies in a continuous field, an Aristotelian has rather a cabinet of natural kinds, species, types, in separate compartments. But science remains a study of species, for knowledge is of the universal. However, the forms come in discrete units here, just as the atoms do in the atomic theory. Causality can be read either as teleological or blindly mechanical. It is probably correct to say, as is often done, that the Aristotelian world-view is the one that would occur naturally to a biologist or a doctor, who studies health and humanity, but health, normalcy, and humanity in individual patients or specimens, each running more or less "true to type."

The fourth pair of commitments, to physical direction and synthetic method, is characteristic of twentieth century process philosophy. It had its classical ancestors—Heraclitus and Anaxagoras come to mind—but it has become a "coordinate force" with the other three families only in our own century. (By this I mean, that it has become a coordinate force as a system of philosophy; poets and mystics have held this metaphysical position continuously, but the tendency has been to treat it as alternative to any "properly philosophical" view until recently.) Process philosophy sees the world as a continuous, dynamic field, with new entities and values emerging with the advance of time. Forms or species are abstractions; explanation depends rather on intuition, on an appreciation of concrete individuals. Where the elements of an atomic theory are separate and static, the single field of a process philosophy is continuous and dynamic. Some students of system call this fourth family "Bergsonian," some "Whiteheadian," and both names are appropriate.

The final tetradic set, then, can be written as a cross, with the vertical axis representing direction; the horizontal, method. This gives:

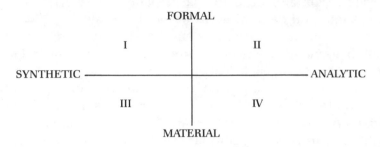

Here, I is Platonic, II is Aristotelian, III is the quadrant of process philosophy, IV is the quadrant of various forms of atomism.

Just in passing, to make this schema more persuasive for readers who are more familiar with fine art than with formal logic, we can compare the sort of structure each of these systems expects to find in the world with one standard way of scoring responses on a Rorschach test. The scoring I have in mind recognizes four types of response: *static* versus *dynamic*, *wholistic* versus *part-by-part*. These four form a tetrad:

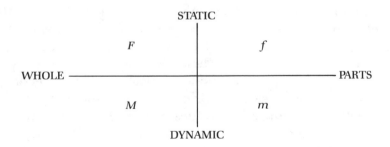

The four correlate beautifully with the systematic presuppositions of the Platonist (*F*), Aristotelian (*f*—or better *fff*), the Bergsonian (*M*), and the atomist (*m*—or, better, *mmmm*). (I have suggested, without persuading anyone, that we could design a test similar to the Rorschach for projected *temporal structure*.)

With very modest modification and translation, my set of systems equals that of Richard McKeon (e.g., in *Freedom and His-*

tory), Paul Weiss (e.g., in *Modes of Being*), Stephen Pepper (his "root metaphors"), Plato (who sets up four "philosophic systems" of these types in the *Sophist*), and Newton Stallknecht (e.g., in Stallknecht and Brumbaugh, *The Compass of Philosophy*).[3]

Each of these formal systems brings with it a different notion of the structure of time, and a different notion of the kind of formal logic most appropriate to reality. This latter point has been developed by Stephan Körner, who points out that one can be "logical" with alternative logics.[4] He distinguishes four types, using two contraries. "*L*" logics ("logistical") are definite and linear; they offer unique causal lines and unique logical entailments; our standard deductive logics are of this type. "*I*" ("intuitionist") logics, on the other hand, give a formal picture of branching sequences leading into a future of different, forking, "options." Where *L* logics match a deterministic world, *I* logics match one with an openness in every future. Both *L* and *I* logics come in two varieties, "common sense" and "technical." The *technical* versions (which Körner abbreviates as *L* and *I*), use sharp analytic definitions to exclude borderline cases. The "common sense" logics (which he abbreviates *L** and *I**), assume a world of *continuity*, in which distinctions tend to blur. Clearly, these four "logics" neatly match my four system families, as a diagram will show.

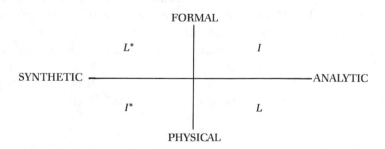

The match is somewhat hidden because the coordinate levels are different. We can re-write this as:

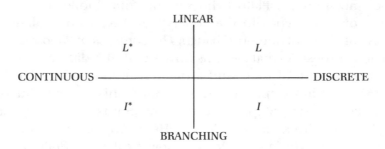

Now, it immediately occurs to any student of the history of philosophy, that since these systems claim to explain the world of our experience, it ought to be possible to test them empirically. Why haven't experiments, over more than two millennia of debate, *confirmed* one or more schemes, and *disconfirmed* the others? Clearly, any such elimination would be a gain for metaphysics. But the awkward historical fact—with consequences for the study of time that I will come to in a moment—is that *all four* have been repeatedly confirmed in the pragmatic world of craft and application. The confirmations, however, take place in different theaters of action for the different systems! Thus, a description of reality as an open field of process exactly matches the view of a creative artist, but the notion of determinate causal chains of elements exactly fits the world of a machinist or applied natural scientist. A mathematician's experience confirms the Platonic, a doctor's or politician's, the Aristotelian, way. It is just here that our basic metaphysical assumption of the applicability of the law of contradiction to time begins to become a liability; for that assumption, plus the facts about systems we have just presented, leads to the conclusion either that three-fourths of our experience is illusion; or that our choices of descriptive frame are equally valid but all alike wholly arbitrary; or that we must give up the law of contradiction totally (and with it, all claim to rationality).

Some interesting light is shed on the tetrads we have discussed by Newton Stallknecht's definitions of the "four tenses" which he associates with the meanings of "is" in his definition of "ontology."[5] These are a past (perfective) tense, a future (inceptive), and *two* "presents," a present eternal (non-temporal), and a present progressive (dividing past from future). Each "tense" exactly fits the theoretic conceptual structure *and* the practical interest of one of my four types of system, logic, and action.

PRESENT ETERNAL	PRESENT PROGRESSIVE
FUTURE (INCEPTIVE)	PAST (PERFECTIVE)

The matrix for *practice* is:

MATHEMATICS LOGIC	MEDICINE POLITICS
FINE ART CREATIVITY	TECHNOLOGY NATURAL SCIENCE

It seems no coincidence that each conceptual system finds its use and confirmation in relation to a *different* aspect of action in time.

It might be well to notice here that Professor Stallknecht is a Whiteheadian, and that I was trained as a literary critic as well as a philosopher. Neither of us would be easily persuaded by an abstract description which failed to match our qualitative intuition. But two decades ago, when I undertook a survey of the *concrete quality* of time as I found it amplified in literature, I found the same fourfold heterogeneity that I have been discussing in the fields of practice and of theory.[6]

For my present purpose, I have selected four works in each of which one set of temporal qualities has been enlarged and presented directly. My four case-studies are Kafka's *Castle*,

Proust's *Remembrance*, Mann's *Magic Mountain* (the middle section), and Sophocles' *Oedipus Rex*. These catch the qualities,
respectively, of a Platonic, an atomic, a process, and an Aristotelian sense of "time"; and do so each by generalizing the properties of one of Stallknecht's aspects or tenses so that it becomes
the entire temporal universe of each myth. A diagram illustrates
the correlation:

KAFKA	SOPHOCLES
(THE CASTLE)	(OEDIPUS REX)
MANN	PROUST
(THE MAGIC	(SWANN'S WAY)
MOUNTAIN)	

Kafka's *Castle* exists, elusive, at the edge of the world of the
Surveyor, K. It is rarefied, almost as though the author had man-
aged to apply a vacuum pump to the temporality of his story.
Not only is the time somehow uneventful, and unmoving, but
its direction is largely arbitrary. If we were to alter the sequence
of episodes, the new ordered mosaics would still illustrate the
same fable. In fact, this notion of a Byzantine mosaic offering
two-dimensional pictures of some allegory may be a comparison
that brings out what I feel to be the distinctive quality of Kafka's
time. Even when a character is in a small waiting-room, watching
the pointless bustle of ledger-bearing angels, we don't know
where the Castle is, who the angels are, or what if anything is
changed by the adventure.[7]

> . . . And when now, after finishing his work in the shed, the coach-
> man went across the courtyard in his slow, rolling walk, closed
> the huge gate and then returned, all very slowly, while he literally
> looked at nothing but his own footprints in the snow—and finally
> shut himself into the shed; and now as all the electric lights went
> out too—for whom should they remain on?—and only up above
> the slit in the wooden gallery still remained bright, holding one's
> wandering gaze for a little, it seemed to K. as if at last those people
> had broken off all relations with him, and as if now in reality he
> were freer than he had even been, and at liberty to wait here in

this place usually forbidden to him as long as he desired, and had won a freedom such as hardly anybody else had ever succeeded in winning, and as if nobody could dare to touch him or drive him away or even speak to him; but—this conviction was at least equally strong—as if at the same time there was nothing more senseless, nothing more hopeless, than this freedom, this waiting, this inviolability. (chap. 8, p. 140)[8]

. . . So, in addition to all his other annoyances, the teacher blamed K. for the cat as well. And that influenced his last words to K., spoken when he reached the door: "The lady has been driven by force to leave this room with her children, because you have re-belliously refused to accept my notice, and because nobody can ask of her, a young girl, that she should teach in the middle of your dirty household affairs. So you are left to yourself, and you can spread yourself as much as you like, undisturbed by the dis-approval of respectable people. But it won't last for long, I promise you that." With that he slammed the door. (chap. 30, p. 176)

. . . "Much more important seems to me the way in which Klamm receives Barnabas. Barnabas has often described it to me, and even sketched the room. . . . It's a room divided into two by a single reading-desk stretching all its length from wall to wall; one side is so narrow that two people can hardly squeeze past each other, and that's reserved for the officials, the other side is spacious, and that's where clients wait, spectators, servants, messengers. On the desk there are great books lying open, side by side, and officials stand by most of them reading. They don't always stick to the same book yet it isn't the books that they change but their places, and it always astounds Barnabas to see how they have to squeeze past each other when they change places, because there's so little room. In front of the desk and close to it there are small low tables at which clerks sit ready to write from dictation, whenever the officials wish it. And the way that is done always amazes Barnabas. . . .(chap. 15, p. 230)

. . . It's not likely to occur to them to look out of the carriage windows in search of petitioners, for the carriages are crammed with papers which they study on the way.

"But," said K., "I've seen the inside of an official sledge in which there weren't any papers." Olga's story was opening for him such a great and almost incredible world that he could not help trying to put his own small experiences in relation to it, as much to convince himself of its reality as of his own existence.

"That's possible," said Olga, "but in that case it's even worse, for that means that the official's business is so important that the papers are too precious or too numerous to be taken with him, and those officials go at a gallop. In any case, none of them can spare time for father. . . ." (Petitions, p. 277)

From Max Brod's Postscript,

. . . This is one of the mysteries and part of the absolute uniqueness of Kafka's art, that for the chosen reader of those great unfinished novels the conclusion loses in importance from the point at which the main assumptions are more or less completely given. . . . (p. 331)

This time has continuity; settings and episodes flow and transform into one another. It has reversibility: as I remarked, an Aristotelian critic would be ill at ease looking for the plot, character, setting; and would probably go away, insisting that this is an *allegory*, not an *epic*. But there is one more thing about this peculiar time, caught beneath the author's magnifying lens, and this, it seems to me, is its weakness of modality. Between waking and dream, actual and possible, there is very little shift of intensity, of color, or of causal coherence.

These three properties capture the quality of the kind of time which I have associated with the metaphysical system of Platonism. And they match the *structural* notion of time as a "fourth dimension"; continuous, and isotropic. In practice, this is the time pattern that a mathematician or a physicist or a cosmologist finds most pragmatically satisfying.

In looking at Plato's astronomy, I found references to four pieces of mechanism, each a model of one level or kind of cosmological "time." The most "realistic" of the four was a static, metal-band model translating pure arithmetical ratio into static geometric circles and radii. By a Platonic law of identity, what stays identical is form, not flow; essence, not existence; structure, not texture. As a result, since forms have a single, present-eternal, modality; an abstract, typical composition; and a causal power that exists at right-angles to becoming; time as anything dynamic, discontinuous, modally divided, is "unreal." In Plato's myths, the effect is to reduce story to allegorical fable, where in fact we get qualitative vividness, but only for so long as we stare at the television screen in the Cave.

The most interesting literary discovery I made when I tried to sort out distinctive intensive time-qualities in literature was that his special treatment of time is responsible for much of the dramatic impact of Sophocles' tragedies. If we think of time as a "now," a present balanced between fixed past and open future, a locus of forced choice, we get a sort of metaphysical counterpart of Sophoclean time. Repeatedly, the drama calls for decision; for fateful decision. In *Oedipus Rex*, this is particularly clear because the discovery and reversal come about from repeated relatively brief crises. The hour has struck; the Messenger been sent for; Tiresias threatened; Apollo's word doubted! Each crisis is irreversible; each offers Oedipus an alternative to his hot-tempered persistence; yet at each point, his character and thought dictate a choice leading to consequences the audience can see. The knife-edge time of Sophocles comes out most clearly in the entrances and exits, the summons and waiting.

I have sent . . ./ Creon, my consort's brother, to inquire / of Pythian Phoebus at his Delphic Shrine / How I might save the state by act or word. / And now I reckon up the tale of days / Since he set forth and marvel how he fares. / 'Tis strange, this endless tarrying, passing strange. / But when he comes, then I were base indeed / If I perform not all the god declares./ CHORUS: Thy words are well-timed; even as thou speakest / That shouting tells me Creon is at hand. (Line 70ff)

Well, I will start afresh and once again / Make dark things clear. . ./ Up, children, haste ye, quit these altar stairs, / Take hence your suppliant wands, go summon hither / The Theban commons. . . . ./(Line 132)

CHO. My liege, if any man sees eye to eye / With our lord Phoebus tis our prophet lord / Teiresias; he of all men best might guide / A searcher of this matter to the light.

OED.: Here too my zeal has nothing lagged, for twice / At Creon's instance have I sent to fetch him, / and long I marvel why he is not here. (Line 285)

OED. (to Teiresias): Must I endure this fellow's insolence? / A murrain on thee! Get thee hence! Begone / Avaunt! And never cross my threshold more. (Line 430)

OEDIPUS AND CREON. CHORUS: I know not; to my sovereign's acts I'm blind / But lo, he comes to answer for himself. OED.: Sirrah, what mak'st thou here? Dost thou presume / To approach my doors, thou brazen faced rogue, / My murderer and the filcher of my crown? (Line 530B)[9]

The same tension carries forward until the final exit ends the play.

Now, this was Aristotle's favorite play. And one reason, I think, is that it exactly matches the analysis of time in practical science which goes with an Aristotelian philosophy. For an Aristotelian can make distinctions, between kinds of time, kinds of change, and kinds of number. The bleak abstract formula of "a number of motion in respect to before and after" hides the concrete diversity of Aristotle's species of time. In theology and astronomy, it is true, time is static: the Prime Mover sees only atemporal reality, the periods of the stars repeat identically, so that the same position becomes before and after. But in his analysis of linear time, Aristotle defines a "now" which divides a fixed past and a modally open future. When this division fails to square with Aristotelian deductive logic, Aristotle changes the logic, to accommodate the sea fight tomorrow. Whenever he works with art, ethics, politics, or history, it is the time of decision that seems to me to be invoked. (At the end of the *Constitution of Athens*, for example, Aristotle sees his story as the account of eleven constitutions and ten revolutions; most of us would have read his data in another way.) Thus Aristotle's enthusiasm for Sophocles reflects, in part, a metaphysical presupposition the two share; one expressing it in the category of quantity, one of quality, but both keenly aware of temporal discontinuity and modality. (Incidentally, this sort of branching sequence matches biological, growth time very well.)

A third quality of time, radically continuous but also radically irreversible, is illustrated by Thomas Mann's *Magic Mountain*. Supposedly, on the top of an enchanted mountain, time would stand still; and Mann's interpolated reflections within the book suggest that he was consciously committed to this sort of enchantment. But the plot itself, as it unfolds, takes on a momentum of its own. From the time that Castorp, entering the sanitorium, notices the clock, calendar, and bell at the reception desk, until the end, when he plunges into a war-torn world in flames, there is a continuous accelerating erosion of structure. As distinctions vanish, one temporal phase blurs into another, and one modality; finally, even the boundary of life and death becomes indistinct. Meanwhile, the protagonist—and the reader—have lost track of days, then of seasons, finally of years: but *not* in Kafka's world of suspended animation. The time in this story has continuity, as radical a continuity as Bergson's *durée*.[10] It also has radical irreversibility: we could define this, if we were minded to draw analogies between science and story, as constantly increasing entropy. But in fact, for our present purposes, at least, it serves better to describe what happens as an increasingly intense capture of the quality of time as directed flow. The reason for my choosing this novel, rather than many others, is the single-mindedness with which this one aspect of time dominates and intensifies. If Sophocles captures the progressive present of crisis, Kafka the present eternal of allegory, Mann in this novel has an inceptive dynamic duration, a captured future. (If one were to try to illustrate this temporal quality by selected *parts* of artistic works, the forward-looking frenetic projects of Alexis Zorba would qualify; so would some sections of Faulkner; and surely many other characters and passages which step into the metaphysics of flow, the "Time" of Heraclitus and Bergson.) This is a time with very interesting scientific implications. On the one hand, it exactly matches the structure needed to explain the biological theory of evolution; on the other, its unpredictable branching and shifting, which escape from our equations, make it a time structure which scientists accept very reluctantly. Just as the time sense of Sophocles is built into his dramatic structure, Mann's rush of time into disorder is not the thing his characters think about on their enchanted mountain, but what they experience. The arrival is factual enough:

> On their right as they entered, between the main door and the inner one, was the porter's lodge. An official of the French type, in the grey livery of the man at the station, was sitting at the telephone, reading the newspaper. He came out and led them through the well-lighted halls, on the left of which lay the reception-rooms. . . . (Number 34, p. 11)[11]

With beautiful continuity, the loss of order proceeds. Hans has a love affair, begun on Walpurgisnacht; his cousin dies; he begins to be disoriented in his thinking about time; he gets lost in the snow. Finally, a seance breaks the barrier between life and death, as the spirit of Joachim returns.

> The record had run off, with a last accord of horns. But no one stopped the machine. The needle went on scratching in the silence, as the disk whirred around. Then Hans Castorp raised his head, and his eyes went, without searching, the right way.
>
> There was one more person in the room than before. There in the background, where the red rays lost themselves in gloom, so that the eye scarcely reached thither, between writing-desk and screen, in the doctor's consulting chair, where in the intermission Elly had been sitting, Joachim sat. It was the Joachim of the last days, with hollow, shadowy cheeks, warrior's beard, and full, curling lips. He sat leaning back, one leg crossed over the other. . . .
>
> But that was no proper uniform he wore. No colour, no decorations; it was a collar like a *litewka* jacket, and sidepockets. . . . And what was it, this headgear? It seemed as though Joachim had turned an army cookpot upside-down on his head, and fastened

it under his chin with a band. Yet it looked quite properly warlike, like an old-fashioned foot-soldier, perhaps. ("Highly Questionable," pp. 855–856)

And, at the end:

What is it? Where are we? Whither has the dream snatched us? Twilight, rain, filth, Fiery glow of the overcast sky, ceaseless booming of heavy thunder; the moist air rent by a sharp singing whine, a raging, swelling howl as of some hound of hell, that ends its course in a splitting, a splintering and sprinkling, a crackling, a coruscation; by groans and shrieks, by trumpets blowing fit to burst, by the beat of a drum coming faster, faster—There is a wood, discharging drab hordes, that come on, fall, spring up again, come on. ("The Thunderbolt," 895–896.)

There is our friend, there is Hans Castorp! We recognize him at a distance, by the little beard he had assumed while sitting at the "bad" Russian table. . . . Look! He treads on the hand of a fallen comrade. . . . (Ibid., p. 898)

For the time quality that matches an atomic theory, where a succession of units or states follow, but each intact and insulated from the rest, we turn to Proust. This peculiar quality of Proust's time sense, with its total recall of unchanged past moments and its total bewilderment at passage is exactly the feeling one would attribute to Zeno's "Arrow."[12] "If I am at every moment at rest in a space equal to my own length," we can imagine the missile asking itself, "when do I move?" Yet the Arrow does collide with the target. Proust has in his memory file an enormous sequence of colored lantern-slides (an image he himself is fond of). They picture things that have changed—yet there is no static slide that pictures change itself. Proust's "atomic" time sense has been repeatedly studied, for example by Georges Poulet.[13] Its association with a metaphysics of separate elements in reversible, discontinuous series, and with a scientific structure of separate sequential moments, is particularly clear. So is the *retrospective* direction in which an author looks when this time quality dominates his work. Only *after the event*, when the immediate impression is recalled as a Humean idea, do we know "what happened." Contrast Marcel to Zorba or to Castorp in this regard; we have the perfective aspect of time confronting the inceptive.

In Proust, we encounter an author whose time sense is dominated by absolute recall. The scenes, flavors, sounds of the past are remembered vividly, unchanging, like magic-lantern slides. What makes *us* change when our world and its time are these atomic essences, snapshots, is a mystery lying outside of the novel, but giving it a plot and direction as the author searches for an answer.

Almost every passage is colored by this retrospective, discrete time quality. For example, *Swann's Way, Overture*, 7.

> Certainly I was now well awake; my body had turned about for the last time. . . . But it was no good my knowing that I was not in any of those houses of which, in the stupid moment of waking, if I had not caught sight exactly, I could still believe in their possible presence; for memory was now set in motion; as a rule I did not attempt to go to sleep again at once, but used to spend the greater part of the night recalling our life in the old days at Combray with my great-aunt, at Balbec, Paris, Doncières, Venice, and the rest; remembering again all the places and people that I had known, what I had actually seen of them, and what others had told me.[14]

The gift of an actual magic lantern for Marcel's bedroom, however, interfered with his own imagination and gave the room an air of unfamiliarity. But he remembers Combray:

> And so it was that, for a long time afterward, when I lay awake at night and revived old memories of Combray, I saw no more of it than this sort of luminous panel, sharply defined against a vague and shadowy background, like the panels which a Bengal fire or some electric sign will illuminate and dissect from the front of a building the other parts of which remain plunged in darkness: broad enough at its base, the little parlor, the dining-room, the alluring shadows of the path along which would come M. Swann, the unconscious author of my sufferings, the hall through which

I would journey to the first step of that staircase, so hard to climb, which constituted, all by itself, the tapering 'elevation' of an irregular pyramid; and, at the summit, my bedroom, with the little passage through whose glazed door Mama would enter; in a word, seen always at the same evening hour, isolated from all its possible surroundings, detached and solitary against its shadowy background, the bare minimum of scenery necessary (like the setting one sees printed at the head of an old play, for its performance in the provinces) to the drama of my undressing, as though all Combray had consisted of but two floors joined by a slender staircase, and as though there had been no time there but seven o'clock at night. I must own that I could have assured any questioner that Combray did include other scenes and did exist at other hours than these. . . . (p. 33)

Pragmatically, the atomic approach to action matches the tools and needs of everyday technology. Arts and crafts are funded human experience, retrospective; mechanisms are series of separate parts, sequential and reversible. But simple and useful as this model is, it cannot account for continuity, modality, irreversibility, mathematics, metaphysics, fine art, or prudence. It competes in, but by no means dominates, the worlds of abstract explanation, of pragmatic action, of intuition and qualitative appreciation.

With this contrast of four immediate qualitative experiences of time, my program of exhibiting tetrads is concluded. Metaphysical presuppositions may be thought of in either of two ways. On the one hand, we may think of schemes of concepts—for example, my schemata of "explanation"—as paradigms which dictate what can be observed. For, if our concepts set limits to what is possible, those limits apply to what is observable as well. On the other hand, we may think of metaphysical orientations as generalizations of familiar modes of action and qualitative perception, extended to cover *all* experience and phenomena though they originate in one part or another of the total field. But, either way, we find alternative presuppositions directing and limiting the study of time. (Nor is the time structure that we choose for each specialized endeavor always the one that is most appropriate.)

We can now return to the very basic metaphysical presupposition that makes us unable to feel at ease with my tetrads.
This is, we recall, the assumption that "time" must be some
single, homogeneous thing; that the law of identity will apply
to it as it would to a physical substance or to a formal structure.
Clearly, if that assumption is right, only one of Richard McKeon's
philosophic schemes, of Stephan Körner's logics, of Newton
Stallknecht's four temporal qualities, of my tetrads of time and
practice, can be "right" or "real." Yet I have just shown that there
is no test which will show one of these alternatives to be real
or right that cannot be used—in a different domain, to be sure—
to support the claims of the other contenders.

But it would be a serious error to draw the conclusion from
the falsity of assumed homogeneity that time is a radically equivocal term. If we decided that each specialist, theoretic, practical,
or poetic, had his own time which had nothing in common with
the other, the result would be like the total chaos that ends
Mann's *Magic Mountain*. Some of us would live in a world where
we backed into a future unaware, contemplating only a fixed
past; others would float in a logical space, like subjects in a
sensory-deprivation tank; and so on.[15] The fact is that "time" is
a complex causal nexus, with different modalities interacting
and intersecting. This was the theme of Paul Weiss's *Modes of
Being*, and though my analysis is not identical with his, I remain
convinced that his central theme was right.[16]

What we find is that "time" involves *four* entities, not one. There
is a frozen, definite linear field of the factual past, where no
possibilities can be found. There is an open, branching or continuous, future domain, where only possibilities lie, and no facts
await us as yet. At the juncture of the two is the Sophoclean
"now": the transformation point that crystallizes future into past,
option into fact, weak disjunction into exclusive alternation.
Overarching these three is the limiting, modally neutral, structural domain of the present eternal: abstract, but setting limits
and offering laws for the contained interacting terrains of passage and change which a mystic or Platonist dismisses as the
appearance, rather than the reality, of time. The Bergsonian,

needless to say, sees the complex the other way, dismissing the abstractions as appearance, looking to intuition to find reality.

What we also find is that there are a dozen metaphysical confusions that can interfere with our sense of time, and can play hob with Conferences such as those of the International Society for the Study of Time. These confusions take the form of substituting one time concept for another, where the substitution is inappropriate, and takes in too much territory. Thus, we might project the closed, deterministic pattern of the eternal present onto the future, and picture ourselves as four-dimensional worms advancing to meet "future facts" already waiting. Or we might project the plasticity of the future onto a past which has in fact set up causal limits for our present options. Wishing the past were corrigible, we might assume it to be; but only a mismatch of expectation and outcome can follow that assumption.

Plato, in the *Parmenides*, proves first that time is nothing, then that it is everything. Both proofs are hypothetical, and neither is right. But the issues they establish are ontological and their dialectic attempts to work through the equations of physics, the canonical forms of logic, the rules of practice, the myths of passage, to capture a vision of the complex reality of time. Once he has captured it, Plato proceeds to dissolve time into a sort of universal solvent of eternity. But I hope my present study of time will be less austere, though not less metaphysical.

Chapter 8
Systems and Tenses:
A Sociology of Time

T HE PURPOSE of this Chapter is to propose three theses which bring together areas of research in philosophy that at present have remained unaware of each other. Whether the result will be illumination or explosion cannot be predicted, but the experiment would, in either case, prove interesting.

My first thesis is that there are exactly four types of philosophic system which recur throughout history; that the four cannot simply be combined by conjunction, for the result of that is contradiction; but that they are related by transformations, hence not totally incommensurable. My second thesis is that all four system types have remained viable because all four work: each is confirmable. But they work perspicuously in different domains of experience; and each works best in a different aspect of time from that which confirms the others. (There are four aspects of time, each with its own appropriate logic, which match the four families of systems.) My third thesis is that the pragmatic result of matching aspects, logics, and systems of met-

125

aphysics can be read as evidence that the four aspects of time are as diverse objectively as the systems and logics that they match.

These theses thus propose bringing together the theme of the study of systems and framework questions, paradigms and root metaphors; that of logics with modes and tenses (since a temporal *aspect* involves both a tense and a mode); and that of ontology, with the highly divergent accounts of "time" offered us by existential and by analytical traditions of contemporary philosophy.[1]

The area of philosophic systems and their classification includes at least three sets of investigations that have not been seen in their proper inter-relation. There is the historical-metaphysical study of philosophic systems; the sort of work Kant programmed in the last chapter of his first Critique. One thinks here of McKeon's philosophical semantics, Pepper's root metaphors, Paul Weiss's four modes of being, G. K. Plochmann's qualifications of simple tetradic taxonomy, and so on. There is the dimension of the philosophy and history of science.[2] In this area, discussion of "paradigms" and their role in structuring observation and explanation serve as a more specific examination of the general "systems" theme. One thinks here of Kordig's recent critique, of Kuhn, Feyerabend, and Toulmin.[3] There is also the area of categorial thinking and formal logic. Here the status of framework questions in logic, given now classical treatment by Carnap and Hempel, is enriched by the construction of alternative logics—with modes, tenses, questions, and so on—which can operate within some, but not all, frames.[4] Stephan Körner's work in category theory is a clear recent formulation of some of the issues and tactics which this logical dimension of system theory involves.[5]

I propose to take up, in turn, the present status, and my theses bearing on it, of the study of systems; the relations of systems and their logics to tenses; and the metaphysical extensions of this relation to an understanding of the nature of time.

Since the Greek Sophists, the differences of major philosophers have been a favorite topic of skeptics, and a persistent annoyance to speculative thinkers and conscientious historians.[8] As a fairly standard classification comes to be accepted, three groups of suggested resolutions appear. The first is an optimistic, "synthetic" treatment. It is assumed that all of the contradictions and divergences are superficial, the result of incomplete attempts to arrive at the same final true and complete philosophy. But when one is asked to state that philosophy, the project turns out to be less a fact than an expressed future-looking hope. For in each period, and indeed within each system that claims completeness, there are well-accredited defenders of contradictory views, and critics eager to show the inner inconsistencies of the supposed total systems.[7]

The second analysis of system relations is "critical." It holds that there is a set of systems, or frameworks, which are mutually exclusive, and that philosophy and science alike presuppose a framework choice. Framework differences cannot be arbitrated or synthesized, nor can the diverse schemes be mutually translated. Ultimately it seems that a choice of frameworks or systems is to be made on the basis of "pragmatic criteria": some schemes are "more useful" than others to attain desired "results." Some of the most interesting work in foundations of logic, philosophy of science, and the history of philosophy has centered on this approach to systematic diversity. Richard McKeon, for example, with his "philosophical semantics," has analyzed historical relations of the statements of philosophers to establish the critical thesis of non-translatability across his four system frames. Rudolph Carnap, in his earlier treatment of external versus internal questions, had suggested—for an unspecified plurality of possible frameworks—that framework choices had to be made on pragmatic grounds. The recent work on "paradigms" in philosophy of science—Kuhn, Toulmin, Feyerabend, Hanson—has explored, and perhaps over-emphasized, the extent to which a conceptual paradigm may control and dictate to observation. From a different, more qualitative and aesthetic standpoint, Stephen Pepper's root metaphors embody the same idea.[8] The "critical" approaches differ in that some claim to tell us what and how many the alternative frameworks or metaphors are, while others seem to admit an indefinite plurality. They agree, however, in recognizing the logical incompatibility of alternative frames, a logical incompatibility which does not admit of some future final conjunction of oppositions as its synthetic resolution.

Perhaps the general similarities of these contemporary approaches to the problem of systems are a reaction against earlier modern assumptions that in fact the contradictions and untranslatabilities were only apparent or only transitory.[9] That attitude was typical of Western systems of the seventeenth century, and again of the Hegelian systems of the nineteenth and early twentieth centuries. In the seventeenth-century version, where truth was treated as non-temporal, the attempts to combine "truths" from different domains resulted in internal contradiction. The classic example is, of course, Descartes' assumption that Augustinian psychology and Galilean physics, each "true" in its own domain, could be simple conjoined within a consistent metaphysical system.[10] This way of tackling the problem came to an end with the critical philosophy of Kant. In the nineteenth- and twentieth-century versions, the assumption was made that truth is the whole, and that its recognition must be evolving and temporal, passing through apparent oppositions in a steady progress. On the one hand, the history of thought seems *not* to match the postulated pattern: the old antinomies remain, and the course is jagged tacking and veering, not neat navigation by some law of dialectic. On the other hand, the postulate of compatibility is bought at the price of certain kinds of logical, physical, and ethical precision: witness the fate of the law of double negation in Hegelian thought. (The notion of alternative systems as reflections of diverse types of *praxis* and *techne* will be discussed later.)

If in fact there have been four and only four families or types of system with any viability in the West, we would expect scholars—metaphysicians and historians—to find equivalent sets of tetrads. And the issue then is whether or not any consistent *transformation*, neither simple conjunction nor simple alternation, related each pair of this group of four. This case has been argued pro and con elsewhere, and is still under debate; Professor G. K. Plochmann and I have recently advocated alternative views, mine being that the fourfold way is indeed the way to understanding system and reality.[11]

Supposing, for the moment, that the case is made for using the fourfold set of types as basis for discussion, the next question might be, why have all four persisted, as we claim they have? Wouldn't it seem much more likely, if indeed we live in a world where metaphysics is possible, that the test of history and the advance of knowledge would permit a *decision*, so that some alternatives would be disconfirmed or would be irrelevant and so drop out? My answer to this, which is one most students of systems would concur in, is that every one of the four system-types has found repeated confirmation.[12] We can't decide between them in that way. It is also true, however, that the areas of experience within which one system is most obviously confirmed are different from those most obviously confirming the others. The case is illustrated nicely by Professor Körner's two logics, his *L* and *I* (logistic and intuitionistic). The *L*-logic has unique causal sequences: the I admits branching "trees" of options. It proves—among other things—pragmatically optimal to use the *L*-logic for description of laws, facts and events in the past, but the *I*-logic gor analysis of present decisions leading into a future.[13] A similar relation holds for the four standard types of philosophy and the four main aspects or tenses of time. Let me define the four types I have in mind here by specifying for each a *direction* of explanation, formal or material, and a *method* of explanation, analytic or synoptic. Platonism is a good term for systems that are formalist in their direction and synoptic in method. Aristotelianism describes an alternative directedness toward form, but toward forms which are individuated and specified, hence treated analytically. Atomism is the class of systems explaining by seeking an underlying material, a plurality of elements which an analytic method discovers. Process philosophy, like atomism, tries to explain by finding underlying spatio-temporal entities; but it is synoptic, joining events and apparent objects in a continuous dynamic field.

By the four main tenses or aspects of time, I refer to another standard classification, one that Professor Newton Stallknecht put particularly clearly in 1950.[14] Time aspects are either past,

or future, or present progressive, or present eternal. The difference between the last two is this: a present progressive is a locus
of choice, a cut in time; the present eternal is proper to a realm
of eternal objects which are immune to variation or change. A
different sort of linguistic and conceptual frame is appropriate
to each temporal standpoint. What hides this correspondence
is our ability to transfer or displace patterns, so that we can talk
about the futures *as though* it were already past, the past *as
though* it were now present, and so on. A peculiarly easy confusion—one which Bergson analyzed well—is the mixing up of
the "is" of the progressive present with the "is" of the eternal.

The match between the conceptual frames and the tenses or
aspects that confirm them is striking. Creativity and novelty,
which process philosophy stresses, are radically future and open
in their time orientation. We are dealing with a field of alternative
creations, not as yet exclusive, and as yet not even definite. For
the creative artist (but not for the critic, as a rule) this prospective
time of process philosophy seems an exact, "realistic" match
with experience. On the other hand, the technician or scientist
working with necessary causal explanations and determinate
observations of fact finds the atomic theory most useful. That
theory is a pattern peculiarly adapted to the full determinateness of facts and causes in the past. For its purposes of explanation, alternative options or fields are irrelevant, and a set of
past facts is the confirming match. For the realm of forms, numbers, and such timeless entities, quite clearly the Platonist's present eternal tense is the one that best describes the networks of
relation and the systems of invariant form. And an Aristotelian
present progressive, with organisms grasping increments of form,
selecting among finite options either consciously or instinc-
tively, offers a time structure which exactly matches the biological concepts of cause and growth, and the ethical idea of choice.

This interesting fact about alternative systems—that each is
clearly applicable, but each to its own proper aspect of time—
suggests a new dimension that system theory ought to explore.
We are becoming familiar enough with logics with tenses to be
able to appreciate the possibility of alternative logical structures

as describing different directions and connections of temporal progress. But by and large, work with tensed logic has gone on independently of work with system theory or with metaphysical analyses of temporality.

Finally, we may come back to the question of the pragmatic grounds for selecting one system rather than another. The ground of empirical confirmation did not decide between them, but suggested that alternative world-views found their clearest confirmation in different areas of experience. It also suggested that what differentiated those areas might well be the time aspect each matched in structure. Now, "pragmatic grounds" imply both a problem and a purpose defining success in its solution. Pragmatically, our frameworks or systems are tools in a box, alternatives awaiting our selection. It takes only modest temerity to suggest that we will be best satisfied when we pick the tool that is best adapted to the objective structure of the problem, which is in turn a function of purpose and of subject matter.

What "works" depends on (1) what I want to do, and (2) when I stand temporally in relation to doing it. I can fail pragmatically because I "want" something inconsistent: for example, I may want to change my behavior of yesterday. I can fail because the tense I pick is possible, but does not match the actual situation. This would be the case if I were to try to inspect and control the future in full detail, misled by my ability to think in future perfect tenses into believing that the future is in fact perfectively structured.

The question, then, of "pragmatic choices" among framework questions may well relate to the other philosophical issues of the structural relations of system types, and the structural correspondence between system types and aspects of time.

With these theses I do not think I am exhibiting any great originality. Rather, I am trying to explore the relation of several sets of topics which have been widely discussed individually, because it seems to me we can profitably investigate at least the possibility of their close interrelation. My standpoint is, pretty clearly, Platonic and metaphysical; but the concerns and questions I have presented have counterparts in every other system frame as well. At least, that is another thesis which seems worth more exploring.

Chapter 9
All Mixed Together:
Time and Metaphor

R ETURNING FINALLY to the investigation of quality with which
our inquiry began, we will look at characterizations of
time by metaphor. For this purpose, I will assume that
literal definitions can also be treated as a limiting case of metaphor—that is, their assertions of *what time is* also count as
statements of *what time is like.*

One thing stands out in this collection: the incredible size and
range of relevant material. It is hard to find *any* quality, substance, process, or sequence that has not, in some context, been
put forward as a symbol of, an analogue of, and a metaphor for,
time.

The mathematical tradition sees time as a field, a fourth dimension. It is a container, within which forms and events are
located by date; it can be mixed with space and in this mixed
form it becomes subject to topological changes (curving, con-
tracting, self-intersecting, and the like). Shelley's dome of many-
colored glass, which stains the white radiance of eternity,

although he uses the image for *life it* could have served equally well for *time*. There is in this image family always a visual quality, a static continuity, and an extension to, and beyond, some far horizon. An ocean can offer an image of time of this sort: Melville's young Platonist in his chapter "At the Masthead" in *Moby Dick* dreams this identification of time, eternity, and sea. Plato himself uses the figure of "an ocean of otherness" to picture a world in chaos, a world of time and space deprived of quantitative structure.[1] Again, the longer periods of the heavens, in their remote cyclic harmony may lend their remoteness and purity to our imagination of temporality. (Seasons and life-cycles, and particularly phases of the moon—shorter, less regular and less remote—catch quite another quality.) Somehow, the flat background of Byzantine fresco, gold coinage, and mosaic, upon which the two-dimensional outlined images of our apparent world are traced and colored, is another such visual projection.[2]

In addition to these metaphors of continuity, infinity, eternity, and invariance is another class that selects and emphasizes the qualities of time that go with life, growth, and shorter natural cycle.[3] The seasons, the moon's phases, the recurring harvest fall in this second category. Time brings maturity, birth and death, and measures growth and age. The epic saga of successive generations of a family, the rise and fall of a civilization—as well as the histories of individual specimens and persons—are what time most truly is if we follow the suggestion of this symbolic family.[4] Geometrically, there is an interesting combination in this sort of time of cycle and straight line. Lives repeat the life-cycle patterns of species, but in successive individuals. Thus, in a way time repeats and circles; but in an epicycle, so that in another way, within the same qualitative category, it is irreversible.[5] In drama, this is time as crisis and decision; in nature—within each cycle—it is time as movement toward *completion* (and beyond, to termination).[6] In this "biological" tradition, it is not surprising that we frequently find personifications of Time, whether as Father figure or not. For example, each New Year brings the pictures once more of the infant year beginning as the aged old year exits from the scene.[7]

An alternative highlighting of the qualities of time associated with it, time as dynamic and irreversible, goes back to Heraclitus's identification of reality with rivers and with fire.[8] The open creative advance of an unending voyage, or of a sine curve generated through geometric space, of an advancing wave pattern of sound or light, all fit in here. The river, chariot, ship, arrow— and Pirsig's motorcycle in *Zen and the Art of Motorcycle Maintenance*—all exemplify this dynamic, continuous, irreversible quality.[9] Time as creation, inquiry, and invention mark this group of selective qualifications. Biological evolution and cosmological expansion replace the static constants and the fixed recurrent cycles that other poets have put before us as the essence of time. Things begin, are created, end, and perish as well as repeat and endure: we look for events of creation and annihilation as well as conservation laws.[10]

A fourth set of metaphors of time centers around the notion of a sequence of static, framed moments. These could be Proust's magic lantern slides.[11] They could be the ticking of a clock, the jump of a stopwatch sweep hand. The scenes framed in the window of a train can represent this quality.[12] Sequence, vibration, enclosure, and theoretical reversibility—or at least practical discontinuity—qualify this world of temporal atomicity. The flashing digital watch is its final capture in technology.[13] Quantum theorists in physics would like to demonstrate a quantum character for physical time, although to do this will require them to find some way around Zeno's paradoxes of The Stadium (with its trains of atom-sized cars) and the Arrow (frozen violence in its knife-edged present moment).

But after all this netting of single specimens, we really seem to come closer to what we are seeking in two-part metaphors of contrast, in which time is at once foreground and background, not exclusively one or the other.[14] The most effective use of such qualitative contrast that I have encountered is the haiku poetry of the sixteenth-century Zen Buddhist monk Bashō. In each of his brief later poems, there is the imagery of a continuous background of some undifferentiated quality, and in the foreground an intrusive, sharply outlined finite temporal object or individual. In "The Temple Pond," the contrast is between the religious, silent, ancient pool and the secular, noisy, transitory frog.

> An ancient temple pool;
> Jump of a frog;
> The sound of water.

But the contrast can be visual, as it is between the orange, mist-filled autumn twilight and a small black cold and huddled crow, in the "Crow on a Bare Bough."

> A solitary crow, perched
> On a bare branch;
> Evening in autumn.

In the West, this pattern has its exponents as well, Conrad, for example:[15]

> The tidal current [of the Thames] runs to and fro in its unceasing service, crowded with memories of men and ships it had borne to the rest of home or to the battles of the sea. It had known and served all the men of whom the nation is proud, from Sir Francis Drake to Sir John Franklin, knights all, titled and untitled—the knights - errant of the sea: It had borne all the ships whose names are like jewels flashing in the night of time, from the *Golden Hind* . . . . to the *Erebus* and *Terror*, on other conquests—and that never returned. *Heart of Darkness*

The search for immortality on the part of a finite but creative being has been a haunting theme of art, adventure, of anticipated peace, since well before Plato's unsurpassed account of Love in the *Symposium*[16]. The forking of a path, without a backward turning, evoked a sense of witchery where three ways meet: the setting of Oedipus's murder of his father, and of a myriad shrines to three-faced Hekate, goddess of the realm beneath the earth. The heavens above, unchanging home for fixed and wandering but returning stars, is alien in one way, but is where we live in another. When someone asked Anaxagoras what his native city was, he pointed to the heavens, and said, "there is my home."[17] Plato's Socrates, in the *Republic*, having outlined his ideal state, tells Glaucon that it is to be found nowhere on earth; but "there is a pattern of it in the heavens; and a wise man will be a citizen of that city, and of no other."[18]

Also, there is the imagery of lottery and chance, sheer luck and fortune against the contrasting backdrop of average normalcy. Perhaps this is best portrayed in the Epicurean notion of "atomic swerve" — a sudden, unpredictable, and uncaused physical discontinuity.[19]

The conclusion I draw is one which was anticipated at the outset. There are definite symbols, metaphors, and imaginative associations which attach to or refer to time. They tend to fall into classes, and are most effective when they are used in pairs that combine internal relatedness and contrast. Those contrasts surely catch the true quality of time. But when we superimpose them or mix them all together, they neutralize each other and into Anaximander's "Boundless" they disappear.

The art, technology, history, and law of nature by which these qualities and contrasts emerge again has been the theme of my earlier discussion in which these aspects have come from the *apeiron* and have been organized by Justice, *katà tēn toū khrónou tặxin,* "according to the order of time."[20]

There are two important conclusions that follow from the preceding considerations.

The first conclusion is that it is a mistake, though a natural and persistent one, to treat time as though it were a single substance, or attribute, or essence. It is, in fact, a transformation relation among three fields of existence, all contained within a neutral fourth domain of being. Entities in different fields have different properties and different logical relations. On the other hand, for some kinds of artificial, mechanical sequences the differences are almost vanishingly slight. And for abstract, atemporal patterns, the differences have been canceled out by the abstraction. Each direction brings with it a different, but relevant, interpretation of causality.

The second conclusion is that a history of the study of time illustrates a repeated type of overgeneralization. In a complex society, we find professionalization; each specialist has a different proper function. By and large, there is some match between individual interests and aptitudes and specializations. Each professional role brings with it a way of seeing, of planning, and of explaining. This is evident from the way in which different aspects of time are selectively emphasized by artists, politicians, priests, and engineers.

Then, by a natural but dangerous step of generalization, each special aspect of time which is *an* aspect is put forward as *the* essence of time, presupposing "time" to be a single thing. (We can see exactly this effect historically as seventeenth-century physics was generalized into a proposed metaphysics in the following centuries. The result of that overgeneralization was to give to the twentieth century—both its "common sense" and its precise "science"—ideas of matter, space, and causality very badly suited to the needs of social science of aesthetics. Each such overgeneralization carries with it the conviction that its relation to other proposed models must be an exclusive one. As long as that conviction holds, there will be lack of appreciation and a running debate among the various specialists—philosophers among them—through intellectual history.

To appreciate this second conclusion, however, requires an unfamiliar act of imagination. For one's familiar personal time sense, whatever one it may be, is not readily tolerant of possible alternatives.

As a clear study in point, let us go back to analysis of time and Aristotle's efficient and final causes. I choose this because I know, from years of teaching Aristotle, that the relation of causality and time involved here can be stated absolutely clearly in the abstract, and yet remain unimaginable for some very able students. The technical point in Aristotle's doctrine is that *after an event* the chain of efficient causes that led up to it is unique and closed. Thus that event, seen retrospectively, is necessary. On the other hand, *before an event*, there are alternative open final causes, and ordinarily there is some contingency. Present choices (conscious or not) connect and transform these domains from one to the other. To me, this seems clear enough. And yet, some of my students insist that they can't imagine it. Some of them argue that *if* the event can be shown to have been necessary retrospectively, then it must have been necessary while it was still in the future. Others argue that *if* there is contingency in the future, there cannot be tight causality in the past. The former group are mostly scientists, the latter humanists. And it is surprising how hard it is, *not* to convert them to Aristotle, but to get them to imagine the causal scheme as he presents it.

The evidence in favor of this second thesis is the analysis offered in the preceding chapters. The conclusion, because it will seem counterintuitive to any professional, needs a very strong defense.

That defense is that alternative philosophic systems, each with a different sort of time, are alike consistent, practically useful, and aesthetically coherent. This is an indirect proof that there is an error in the implicit assumption that the systems must be *exclusive* alternatives.

We must remember, though, that while each system can claim the pragmatic virtue of "working," each "works" best in a different domain. And this underscores the point that it is wrong to assume that there is only a single time orientation suited to the level of practice. Further, since if there were only one correct metaphysical system, there would be only one "realistic" practical temporal structure, this observation also tells against the assumption of system exclusiveness.

I must emphasize the fact that my suggestion that professions have their own time orientations is not a reduction of philosophy or physics to sociology. On the contrary, the sociological effect results because the metaphysical situation is the one I have described.

Let me conclude with a retrospective summary. Chapter 1 introduces the notion—by an inspection of appearance—that there are four very different kinds of things, and kinds of philosophic definitions of them, that constitute the extension of the term "time."

Chapter 2 offers a brief preliminary look at the relation of time to pattern, process, and space. It notes that time as process does not reduce to time as mathematical dimension or abstract formal pattern, though the Platonic tradition favors such a reduction.

Chapter 3 takes up the theme of chapter 1 again, not on the general level of phenomena, but more specifically in the sphere of mechanics: hardware for defining and measuring time by models of it. This is today so complex a topic that chapter 3 simplifies it by going back to the models which, it seems, Plato used or referred to in his Academy. Even in that early stage, I find four alternative models, each catching one of the aspects of time that defined the families of phenomena; and the four models are so related that no mechanical synthesis of them into a single supermodel is possible.

Chapter 4 explains the Platonic thesis that the kinds of time result from deviations from a pure Form of Time, deviations coming from admixture of degrees of unreality. The divided line of Plato's *Republic* is used as the schematism of this reality-to-appearance descent of time, from pure dimension to cacophonic linguistic fragmentations.

Chapter 5 explores the logic of planning and calculating in systems that use propositions with tenses. It turns out that the most ingenious strategy the author can devise still will not fuse the logic applying to propositions in the realm of form (propositions, that is, as Whitehead and Russell treat them in *Principia Mathematica*), and propositions in the realm of cosmology—or, less grandiosely, the realm of the desk calendar as opposed to the truth table—(it is in this latter sense that Whitehead treats propositions in *Process and Reality*).

Chapter 6 moves to an analysis of choices in a temporal progressive present, and the relation of such choices to values. The chapter suggests that an ethical theory can follow from a proper understanding of present time and a new formal model for comparisons of value.

Chapter 7 returns once more to the thesis that there are four types of philosophic systems, and, matching these, four kinds of time. (It is thus located on the top level of the Platonic divided line in its demand for a final synoptic vision.) This chapter argues that it is a mistake to think of time as being, or even as denoting, a *single* substance, structure, or quality. If it were anything like these, we could decide between the alternative systematic definitions by some test of consistency, or of efficiency and confirmability, or aesthetic and intuive intensity and evidence.

Chapter 8 moves back down the divided line to the world of society and nature. With civilization comes specialization; and specialization involves selective attention. Ordinarily, each specialized profession has its own scheme of concepts, and each brings with it a privileged time orientation. This suggests that the genetic explanation of the different time definitions, and perhaps even of the different philosophic systems, may lie here. For it is easy to overgeneralize, creating a whole metaphysics by assuming that the concepts and categories that work for me when I am seriously engaged in my profession are the only ones that will work for anyone. But this genetic postscript does not pose as *noetic* or *dianoetic* explanation.

Finally, Chapter 9 returns to the world of appearance with which we began; this time, to that world as it is observed by sensitive poets, whose metaphors catch the essential qualities of time in fine art. Through an amazing range of examples, with the greatest sensitivity in their presentation, we can explore this theme of temporality in literature. Each metaphor, each set of metaphors, for time is absolutely convincing: there is no doubt of the depth of insight they express. Only, when we try to construct a single, superbrilliant aesthetic metaphor by a superposition of them all, the mixture we bring together comes out a neutral gray, like the boundless of Anaximander. (Or, on a more homely level, like the gray or muddy brown color that results when someone, hoping for a new level of beauty, dips an Easter egg into too many successive colors.)

As I have said, my conclusion is that this extension of selectively applicable categories to the whole of reality is, however natural, an error. It is a case of taking in too much territory— like the fallacy of illicit process in syllogistic logic. Of course, intelligence not only does, but should, constantly try for increased generality. But intelligence must also constantly check its generalities, particularly when there seem to be equally plausible competing alternatives. (For example, the notion that all geometry must be Euclidean geometry is an overgeneralization. But this did not, for a long time, occur to geometers even when they found that alternatives to the Parallel Postulate led to no inconsistencies. This mutual consistency in the face of a tacitly presupposed incompatibility frustrated a classical tradition, discussed by Proclus, and such a talented modern mathematician as Saccheri.)

I believe we are in a situation in the study of time comparable to that of the recognition of non-Euclidean geometries in the study of space. But I am afraid that for some while to come, my arguments will be regarded as Saccheri regarded his own discovery of non-Euclidean geometry.

Notes

Introduction

1. There are some developments that are more promising than this suggests, but the logic of "implies aesthetically" remains well beyond them.

2. This, however, as my discussion will show, turns out to be just as ambiguous and unsatisfactory as the search for the right mathematical model. An extraordinary variety of alternative calendars and clocks, and an equal variety of explanatory metaphors, confounds the attempted retreat to a simple technological or a subtle aesthetic definition.

3. See my *Whitehead, Process Philosophy, and Education* (Albany, 1982); and chap. 5, below.

4. See below, chap. 5, "Propositions." It is very hard to convince formalists that we cannot construct existence from sufficiently complex essence; and in fact, I tried that misguided operation in 1965, in a formal construction that constitutes the second section of this chapter.

5. Chap. 4, "Passage," below.

6. H. Hesse, *Journey to the East*, trans. H. Rosner (New York, 1957), 107–18; *Steppenwolf*, trans. B. Creighton (New York, 1963), 202–34, 242–46; *Siddhartha*, trans. H. Rosner (New York, 1951), 133–39, 151–53.

Chapter 1. Kinds of Time

This chapter draws upon my article "Kinds of Time: an Excursion in First Philosophy," originally published in *Experience, Existence, and the Good: Essays in Honor of Paul Weiss* (Southern Illinois University Press) 1967, 119–26.

1. See the Bibliography section, "Time Sense and Time Estimation," in Gay Gaer Luce, *Biological Rhythms in Human and Animal Physiology* (New York, 1971), 183; of particular interest here is R. Ornstein, *On the Experience of Time* (Harmondsworth, 1969). From another perspective, G. Poulet, *Studies in Human Time* (Baltimore, 1975).

2. A. Einstein, *The Meaning of Relativity*, 3d ed. (Princeton, 1955), 2.

3. It seems we need to bring to our science some intuitive judgments either of simultaneity or uniform velocity.

4. Classical atomism: see, for example, C. Bailey, *The Greek Atomists and Epicurus* (Oxford, 1928); Descartes, *Meditations*, trans. Haldane and Ross (Cambridge, 1968).

5. Cf. J. Callahan, *Four Theories of Time in Ancient Philosophy* (Cambridge, 6. Aristotle, *Poetics* 1450a36.

7. For the current state of cosmology, described nontechnically, cf. *Scientific American: Cosmology + 1*, with an introduction by Owen Gingerich (San Francisco, 1977).

8. For Plato's formula, *Timaeus* 38A. Cf. Callahan, *Four Theories of Time*; Plotinus, *Enneads* 1, 2, 3; R. Brague, *Du temps chez Platon et Aristote* (Paris, 1982).

9. For a process notion of a "field," as opposed to an abstract mathematical "dimension," see my "Space: Neither Void nor Plenum," *Process Studies* 7 (1979): 161–72.

10. Plato, *Parmenides* 155C.4.

11. Cf. Plotinus, *Enneads* 3.8, 4.8.

12. George Orwell, *1984*; and cf. Bertrand Russell's comments on Dewey's theory of truth, "John Dewey," chap.30 in *A History of Western Philosophy* (New York, 1945), 811–19.

13. See below, chap. 8, "Metaphysical Systems."

14. For Bashō, see H. Henderson, *Introduction to Haiku* (New York, 1958).

Chapter 2. Abstract Pattern and Concrete Process

1. S. Pepper, *World Hypotheses* (Berkeley, 1947); N.P. Stallknecht and R.S. Brumbaugh, *The Compass of Philosophy* (New York, 1952).

2. A. N. Whitehead, *Science and the Modern World* (New York, 1952).

3. My *Whitehead*, 37–48, discusses this.

4. Reports of "W" observers: Whitehead, "The Romantic Reaction," chap. 5 in *Science and the Modern World*; A. N. Whitehead, "Metaphor," chap. 10 in *The Concept of Nature* (Cambridge, 1920; reprint, Ann Arbor, 1957).

5. "Thus the character of a moment and the ideal of exactness which it enshrines do not in any way weaken the position that the ultimate terminus of awareness is a duration with temporal thickness." Whitehead, "Time," chap. 3 in *Concept of Nature* , 69.

6. Whitehead, "The Romantic Reaction."

7. Whitehead, "Abstraction," chap. 11 in *Science and the Modern World*.

8. See chap. 2 of my *Whitehead*.

9. Whitehead had an idea here that I do not find developed in his later works. "All aesthetic experience is feeling arising out of the realization of contrast under identity. . . . In the physical world, this principle of contrast under an identity expresses itself in the physical law that vibration enters into the ultimate nature of atomic organisms." *Religion in the Making* (New York, 1926), 115–16.

10. N. M. Lawrence, "Whitehead: The Rhythm of Nature," in R. S. Braumbaugh and N. M. Lawrence, *Philosophers on Education* (Boston, 1963), 154–85; N. M. Lawrence, "Nature and the Educable Self in Whitehead," *Educational Theory* 15 (1965): 205–16.

11. A. N. Whitehead, *Adventures of Ideas* (New York, 1933); George Allan, "A Whiteheadian Approach to the Philosophy of History" (diss., New Haven, 1973).

12. Reason aims at three things: "living; living well; and living better." A. N. Whitehead, *The Function of Reason* (Princeton, 1929).

13. It seems that there cannot be fully concrete repetition in the world of process philosophy. The appearance to the contrary is due either to substituting an abstract outline for the concrete events and occasions in question, or using a metric scale too short to pick up the slight differences that constitute reiteration over a cumulative longer period.

14. Joseph Conrad, *The Secret Agent* (London, 1920).

Chapter 3 Images and Models

This chapter draws upon my article "Plato and the History of Science," originally published in Studium Generale by Springer Verlag 1961, 520–22.

1. An operationalist holds exactly this view. In general, a physicist would agree with Einstein that a definition of something in physics is not very relevant until it specifies some way to measure the thing defined.

2. G. J. Whitrow, *The Natural Philosophy of Time*, rev. ed. (Oxford, 1981); H. Bondi, *Relativity and Common Sense* (New York, 1962).

3. Ornstein, *On the Experience of Time*. See the Bibliography in Luce, *Biological Rhythms*, 183.

4. Derek Price, *Science Since Babylon* (New Haven, 1961); G. H. Baillie et al., eds., *Britten's Old Clocks and Watches and their Makers,* 7th ed. (New York, 1956). The latter is a fascinating book for anyone who likes clocks, gadgets, and ingenious mechanisms; it has an excellent bibliography.

5. See below, chap. 4.

6. The trouble is that our thousands of ways of measuring time give us increments that don't coincide or correlate. A preview of this problem — reflecting a lack of consideration of human convenience on the part of nature — shows up in the history of the calendar. Somehow days, phases of the moon, seasons measured by lengths of days, years timed by the sun compared to years timed by the stars, offer a very complex set of problems. Increasing civilization increases the complexity.

7. In the following discussion, I am indebted to my colleagues Professors Rulon Wells and Derek J. de Solla Price for many helpful criticisms and suggestions.

8. *Republic* 7. 522B.4

9. Spinning in *Republic* 10; spinning and weaving, *Statesman*; carpentry, *Philebus*; ore refining, *Statesman*; instrument making, *Timaeus* 35 (as interpreted below); medicine extensively in the *Timaeus*; a potter's wheel, *Republic* 5; trireme reinforcing, *Republic* 10, an eel-trap, *Timaeus*; etc.

10. *Republic* 7. 529E ff.; and see the four passages discussed in detail below.

11. *Statesman* 268D-274D.

12. *Timaeus* 47A ff.; the problem is the apparent operation of the mirror shown in figure 88 of my *Plato's Mathematical Imagination* (Bloomington, 1954; hereafter cited as *PMI*), 234; and see ibid., viii.

13. See particularly A. Rivaud, "Études platoniciennes; I. Le système astronomique de Platon," *Rév. d. Hist. d. Phil.* 2 (1928): 1–26; P.-M. Schuhl, "Sur le mythe du Politique," *Rév. de Met. et de Morale* 39 (1932): 47–58. See A. E. Taylor, *A Commentary on Plato's Timaeus* (Oxford, 1929); and F. M. Cornford, *Plato's Cosmology* (New York, 1937), notes on *Timaeus* 35A ff.; also *PMI*, 294–95 n.11, for technological interpretations of this "cutting."

14. P.-M. Schuhl, "Autour du fuseau d'Ananké," *Rev. Archéologique* 2 (1950): 58ff.

15. Taylor, *Commentary*, 161–62 n. 2, poses the problem; for the "law of nines" development see J. Cook Wilson, "Plato *Republic* 616E," *Classical Review* 16 (1902): 292–93; J. Adam, *The Republic of Plato*, 2 vols. (Cambridge, 1902), 2:470–79; R. S. Brumbaugh, "Colors of the Hemispheres in Plato's Myth of Er (*Republic* 616E)," *Classical Philology* 46 (1951): 173–76; R.S. Brumbaugh, "Plato, *Republic* 616E: The Final 'Law of Nines,'" *Classical Philology* 49 (1954): 33–34.

16. *Statesman* 270A.9.

17. *Statesman* 369E.

18. *Timaeus* 33D.

19. *Statesman* 274E. See J. B. Skemp, *Plato's Statesman* (New Haven, 1954), notes on this passage.

20. *Timaeus* 36C-D; 48A. See, in connection with the latter passage, Cornford, *Cosmology*, 361–64.

21. CIcero, *De republica* 1, xiv; cited in Price's study of clockwork; see below.

22. *Timaeus* 22D introduces the "parallax"; for the dismissal of astrology, ibid., 40D, and cf. Cornford, *Cosmology*, 135 n. 1.

23. *Timaeus* 35A ff.

24. Cornford, *Cosmology*, frontispiece; for the fusion of metaphors in the construction, cf. *PMI* 221–30.

25. *Timaeus* 40C.1ff.

26. Ibid. This is a notoriously difficult passage; the four alternatives mentioned need further study.

27. This is the reason for Plato's fusion of his metaphors from technology and mathematics with the motif of "the music of the spheres."

28. In fact, a moving model would be less effective as a representation of eternal invariants regulative of cosmic structure.

29. On books and reader in Plato's time, see the interesting observations of E. G. Turner, *Athenian Books in the Fifth and Fourth Centuries B.C.* (London, 1952). Against the argument that the world-soul ratios are too technical and exotic for a general audience to construct, compute, or appreciate, see *PMI*, 227.

30. *Republic* 6.509D ff.

31. Taylor, *Commentary*, 244–45; A. Rivaud, ed., *Platon, Timée, Critias*, Budé ed. (Paris, 1925).

32. G. Schmidt, ed., *Pneumatica et automata*, vol. 1 of *Heronis Alexandrini opera*, 6 vols. (Leipzig, 1899–1903).

33. Derek J. de Solla Price, *On the Origin of Clockwork, Perpetual Motion Devices, and the Compass*, Paper 6, Contributions from the Museum of History and Technology, *United States National Museum Bulletin* 218 (Washington, D.C., 1959).

34. Derek J. de Solla Price, "An Ancient Greek Computer," *Scientific American*, June 1959, cover illustration, 60–67.

35. The well-shaft for the floating weight would presumably be refilled rapidly from a large sluice; and the globe would spin backward as the well-shaft filled.

36. Schmidt, *Pneumatica et automata*; pseudo-Aristotle, *Mechanica* 848a20ff.; Plato, *Euthyphro*, 11C.3; *Meno* 97D.9; etc.

37. Schuhl, "Ananké"; see n. 9, above.

38. *Epinomis* 984B; *Laws* 903B.

39. J.Burnet, *Early Greek Philosophy*, 4th ed. (London, 1938), 304 n. 1.

40. The simplicity of the integral ratios which have explanatory power in natural science and which give us the structure of the musical scale would thus represent a convergence, in the Platonic model, of symmetry and beauty

as keys to truth (so far as natural science can attain truth). Compare *Philebus* 66B.

41. *Republic* 7.529E; *PMI*, 104–7.

Chapter 4. A Descent into Unreality

1. H. Bergson, *Introduction to Metaphysics*, trans. T. Hulme New York, 1912).

2. The desire for return is a constant theme in Plotinus and Proclus. In connection with the latter, see R. Klibansky's note on the *Commentary in the Parmenides*, in Klibansky and Labowsky, eds., *Plato Latinus III*, (London, 1953), 87–88.

3. Proclus, *Commentary in Parmenides*, in V. Cousin, ed., vol. 4 of *Opera* (Paris, 1821). For the end of the Seventh Book, see Klibansky and Labowsky, *Plato Latinus III*, 26–27. "For by means of a negation, Parmenides has removed all negations. With silence he contemplates the One." *Plato Latinus III*, 77.

4. Leibniz seems to have anticipated a mathematics of *situs*, place. The question is, what properties will remain invariant if a continuous space, containing figures or series, has its metric properties deformed, and has its curvature changed. For an introductory statement of the modern branch of mathematics, see Courant and Robbins, *What is Mathematics?* (Oxford, 1941).

5. Plato's treatment of astronomy, as well as his other discussions of time, contain references both to models and to the technological processes (mixing, measuring, cutting, bending, joining, spinning) of their construction.

6. *Timaeus* 32A; the soul is made by blending Being, Same and Other; subsequently, it is given Motion.

7. That the form of time is not identical with phenomenal time follows directly from the basic assumptions of Plato's theory. In the same way, an equation expressing a form of flow is not itself flowing.

8. See below, chap. 6.

9. Number theory: *Republic* 7.525B ff.; and the scholion to *Charmides* 165E. See Sir T. Heath, *History of Greek Mathematics* (Oxford, 1921) 1: 13–16.

10. *Republic* 7 gives Plato's specifications of a "pure" mathematical astronomy. See A. P. D. Mourelatos, "Plato's 'Real Astronomy': *Republic* 527D-531D," in *J. P. Anton, ed., Science and the Sciences in Plato* (New York, 1980), 33–73.

11. Cf. *Republic* 8. 546A: "For everything that comes into being, there is a period of decay. . . ."

12. Aristotle's detailed treatment, *On Youth and Age*, in the *Parva Naturalia* gives a classical statement of this theme.

13. For the six-minute clock, see my note in *Ancient Philosophy* 1. (1981): 82.

14. Aristotle thought this was no problem. But to account for the subordinate cyclic motions, he needed "either 47 or 55" subordinate prime movers.

15. Sosigenes as quoted by Proclus, W. Kroll, ed., vol. 2 of *Commentarium in Rem Publicam* (Amsterdam, 1965), 23ff.

16. It is fascinating to see a reflection of this tension in early Indian astronomy. There seems a conviction that there must be some largest cosmic period, but an equally strong belief that no given finite age, however large, can be this limit. This leads to calculations of exponentially increasing periodic "ages" running far beyond Sosigenes' 33 trillion years.

17. See below, chap. 5, for a logic with tenses.

18. For a discussion of repetition versus reiteration, see my *Whitehead*, 40–46.

19. For a fascinating survey of contemporary work with biological time, see Luce, *Biological Rhythms*.

20. Ornstein, *On the Experience of Time*.

21. This comparison of Hesse's novel and Plato's dialogue first occurred to me in writing my *Plato on the One* (New Haven, 1961), where it is stated briefly in 32–33 n. 37.

22. H. Bergson, *Time and Free Will*, trans. F. M. Pogson (London, 1920), 191–98.

23. This is one of his central points, ibid., n. 22.

24. Or, at the very least, subjective time preserves the relation of "between" for the states and events it contains; it does not introduce cuts which alter this relation.

25. These linguistic devices certainly operate in the cases I can check at first hand, various Indo-European languages and literary Japanese. But my claim is that these, or equivalents to them, are a practical necessity for *any* language. Historically, it seems that it is *completedness* to which languages have paid most attention; but there are traces of other ways of setting up aspects and tenses, so that the primitive pessimism and fatalism of the world of the perfect tense is not the only one possible for an effective language system.

26. The widespread use of digital watches and clocks gives an intuitive and practical content to this. In the discussion of D. Corish's paper, "Time, Space and Freewill: the Leibniz Clarke Correspondence" (*International Society for the Study of Time Proceedings* 3: 635–53), it was suggested that given their choice, Leibniz's God would be delighted by the new digital watches (with time flashing past in moments of fulguration), where Clarke's deity would insist on a railroadman's accurate analogue timepiece. This discussion, unfortunately, did not find its way into the *Proceedings* except for a tangential reference in my comments on the paper (*Proceedings* 3: 656–57).

27. See M. Čapek, *The Philosophical Impact of Contemporary Physics* (New York, 1961); and Andrew G. Bjelland, "Evolutionary Epistemology: Čapek and the Bergsonian Tradition," (Center for Process Studies, 1981, mimeographed).

28. In a world of moments and states, there is another difference. Where the number series consists of a set of actual terms that extend indefinitely in the "greater than" direction, the moment series consists of the present and an actual past-to-present series, but the future is not yet actual, so the series of actual moments always stops abruptly in the "$t+$" direction.

29. The human soul is created as a mixture of Being, Same, and Other: *Timaeus* 41D.

Chapter 5 Propositions

This chapter draws upon my article "Applied Metaphysics: Truth and Passing Time," originally published in *The Review of Metaphysics*, 1966; 647–66.

1. See Charles Bigger, *Participation* (Baton Rouge, 1968).

2. C. I. Lewis and C. H. Langford, *Symbolic Logic* (New York and London, 1932).

3. A. N. Whitehead, *Process and Reality* (New York, 1929; corrected ed., New York, 1978).

4. D. Sherburne, "Reason and the Claim of Ulysses: A Comparative Study of Two Rationalists, Blanshard and Whitehead," *Idealistic Studies* 4 (1974): 18–34.

5. Whitehead, *Process and Reality* (corrected ed.), chap. 9, sec. 6, 203–5.

6. The need for a new connective to represent causality is generally recognized.

7. The project of generating becoming from being is a tempting one. I thought I might have done it with my logic with tenses in 1967. But, as I will show in a later discussion of passage, there is always an addition of some kind of unreality involved in the process.

8. *Ennead* 5. 12. 9.

9. For the immunity of mathematics to experimental correction, cf. Kant, *Prolegomena to Any Future Metaphysics*. Plato, in the *Theaetetus*, makes an equivalent point in showing the impossibility of equating errors in arithmetical process with deductions in number theory.

10. Russell makes this point in his criticism of Dewey's theory of truth, "John Dewey," 819–28.

11. For Whitehead's proposed new, more general, "aesthetic" symbolic logic see "Analysis of Meaning" in *Essays in Science and Philosophy* (New York, 1948), 93–99: "We must end with my first love — Symbolic logic. When in the distant future the subject has expanded ... I suggest that Symbolic Logic ... will become the foundation of aesthetics. From that stage it will proceed to conquer ethics and theology. ..." p. 99. See also "On Concrete Seeing" in my *Whitehead*, 85–96, esp. 92–93.

12. *Ibid.*, 91–96.

13. For the calendar, see A. Rehm, "Parapegma," in Pauly-Wissowa, *Realencyclopädie* (Stuttgart, 1949), 18:4: 1295–1363.

14. Thus engagements are a third kind of thing, neither facts nor pure nonfacts.

15. The comparison of calendar advance to biological growth is frequent in common speech and poetry. For example, New Year's Day sees the replacement of the Old Year by the New.

16. J. Hall et al., *Criminal Principles and Procedures* (Indi .apolis, 1976).

17. For a sharper definition of "non-facts," see the treatment of "non-conformal propositions" in Sherburne, "Reason and the Claim of Ulysses."

18. See below "An Appendix on Logic and Passage."

19. See my *Ancient Greek Gadgets and Machines* (New York, 1965).

20. Heron of Alexandria, in the 2nd century A.D., has diagrams and descriptions: *Pneumatica et automata.*

21. See my "Space: Neither Void nor Plenum," *Process Studies* VII (1979), 161–72.

22. See my *Whitehead.*

23. But for more technical aspects of passage, see above, chap. 5.

24. David Hume, *Enquiry Concerning Human Understanding*, ed. C. W. Hendel (New York, 1955); H. Bergson, *Time and Free Will*, trans. F. L. Pogson (London, 1920).

25. This is the retrospective situation for Aristotelian "efficient causes."

26. This is Aristotle's view; see, in particular, *Metaphysics* Theta.

27. This stipulation, that a proposition has a fixed truth value, makes for elegance and efficiency in logic. It is taken as a principle by "Aristotelian" logicians. Aristotle himself, however, recognized several classes of exceptions.

28. One metaphysical account of this status is Whitehead's notion of "partially conformal propositions," discussed in the present chapter.

29. M. Heidegger, *Platons Lehre von der Wahrheit* (Berlin, 1942), Pepper, *World Hypotheses.*

30. In different ways, Bergson and Dewey concur in denying any status to supposed "future facts."

31. Whitehead, *"Importance," The Function of Reason.*

32. See Peter A. French, ed., *Philosophers in Wonderland* (St. Paul, 1975).

33. Another account of these is given in the preceding chapter.

34. Aristotle, on Archytas's rattle, *Politics*, 1340b26.

35. This resolution weakened, however; see above, the discussion of time and language in the preceding chapter.

36. I wonder why there has been no attempt to follow out this suggestion that there are *alternative* patterns of truth value change with time for a different sorts of statement.

37. Sherburne, "Reason and the Claim of Ulysses," 18–34.

38. Whitehead, *Process and Reality*, pt. 3, chap. 4.

39. Professor Cobb's comments were made at the Conference on Whitehead's Philosophy in Relation to Education, Center for Studies of Process Philosophy, Claremont, Calif., in 1980.

40. This is equivalent to Stephan Körner's 'I' logic; see chap. 8, below.

41. For Aristotelian propositions of "indeterminate quantity" see *De Interpretatione*, 19b20–30, 17b1–25. A similar approximate quantification was used by Robert Hartman in his formal axiology, to indicate the relative approximation of an instance to an ideal concept: *The Structure of Value* (Carbondale, Ill., 1967), 210ff.

42. This means, if we were to represent input of experience as a curve, that it must be *changes in the third derivative* which are the potential points of division. Borrowing terms from E. M. Berkely, we can call a unified single experience a "state" and a dividing point an "event." Then this condition becomes a definition of states and events: for states $dI^3 / d^3T = k$; for events, $dI^3 / d^3T \neq k$. (I is intensity, T is clock-time.) An important pair of corollaries follows. First, while we cannot force anyone to "pay attention" to the potential divisions in an environmental change, we *can* construct situations which are intrinsically monotonous, because they lack any potential points where they could be so divided. Second, when we try to counteract monotony by any *planned regular change* (continuous shifting of sound, position, lighting) we run the risk, if dI^2 / d^2I is constant, of *increasing it*.

Chapter 6. Decisions

This chapter draws upon my article "Changes of Value Order and Choices in Time," originally published in *Value and Valuation: Essays in Honor of Robert Hartman* (University of Tennessee Press), 1972, 49–63.

1. Hartman, *The Structure of Value*.

2. The utilitarian additive rule is that every increment of pleasure is equal to every other, no matter whose pleasure it is. And the best course of action is defined as "the greatest pleasure and utility for the greatest number."

3. "This is how a man who hopes to win lasting fame on the field of battle should behave, and not care for his life." *Beowulf*, trans. David Wright (Harmondsworth, 1957), 63. Cf. p. 71: "Loaded with gold, Beowulf left him, and crossed the fields exulting over the wealth that he had won." Plato (?), *Alcibiades* 1. 115D: "I would give up life itself if I had to be a coward" (Loeb trans.).

4. See my "Space: Neither Void nor Plenum."

5. Some details of value calculation, with a new model, follow below.

6. Hartman, *The Structure of Value*.

7. Plato, *Statesman* 283D ff.

8. Plato's details of Atlantis, where the scale was everywhere too large, are spelled out in the *Critias*.

9. Hartman, *The Structure of Value*; and my "Formal Value Theory: Transfinite Ordinal Numbers and Relatively Trivial Practical Choices," *Journal of Human Relations* 21 (1973).

10. G. Cantor, *Contributions to the Founding of the Theory of Transfinite Numbers*, trans. P. Jourdain (reprint, New York, 1955).

11. Plato,*Statesman* 283D ff.

12. P. R. Halmos, *Naive Set Theory* (New York, 1960).

13. An earlier brief statement of my project of adding transfinite ordinals to the model was given in my article cited in n. 9, above. Robert Hartman replied, "Reply to Eckhardt and Brumbaugh," *Journal of Human Relations*: 220–26. He said: "I agree with the importance of using transfinite ordinal numbers and have used them in exactly the way Brumbaugh proposes, but without elaborating this use the way Brumbaugh does, and which I fully accept." But his reference (*Structure of Value*, 204) is a text that *does not* use the ordinals in the way I do. Instead, they are there used to rank *stratified levels* of mystical or rational "insight." And, indeed, it is clear from the next page that Robert Hartman did not want to use these numbers in the way that I do. For he wrote (p. 223): "In value theory, as far as I am concerned, there are no trifles."

14. See "On Concrete Seeing" in my *Whitehead*.

15. Above, chap. 6.

16. There are various options for handling negative values; the one chosen will not change the present argument.

17. Aristotle's logic of indefinite quantity, *De Interpretatione* 17b1–25, 19b20–30. Axtell (Cambridge, 1968); *Of Education*, sec. 115, pp. 226–27; *Of Study*, sec. 4, pp. 409–10.

19. Plato, *Republic* 6. 508A–509E.

20. Cf. the United States Declaration of Independence.

21. Logical: Kant; aesthetic: Whitehead; prudential: Bentham, Mill.

22. Kant, *Fundamental Principles of the Metaphysics of Morals*, trans. L. W. Beck (New York, 1959).

23. Cf. J. P. Sartre, *Existentialism*, trans. B. Frechtman (New York, 1947).

24. It is odd that Kantian moralists have not noticed that the fact that ethical imperatives do not extend to interests in effect guarantees an *ethical*—not necessarily a political or aesthetic—moral right to style.

25. Thus we *ought not* to treat differences in interest as a *moral* issue. Whether a Kantian would care to go beyond this, and argue that preserving dignity and self-identity for a being with a sense of beauty and capacity for enjoyment requires us — if we are consistent — never to choose the ugly or painful of a pair of options is an interesting question, but one we will not now pursue.

26. Descartes's 4th rule of method, *Discourse*, pt. 2, rule 4.

27. The "progress" patterns are interesting in connection with the present "generation gap." Material and social resources, as well as essences, serve as necessary conditions for value realization. Thus, although they are in their noninstrumental role of order S, by the principle of limitation they count as equal to the higher orders that require them. (This situation is the key to much modern political debate: one group of theorists stresses that S and E conditions

are *necessary* for realization of intrinsic value; another group stresses that they are *not sufficient*. Both are right.) But with increasing rates of technological and social change, new alternatives keep appearing: what were once necessary limits now become arbitrary limitations. An older generation tends to begin planning *within* the assumed limits that held earlier; a younger generation, which has seen these limits constantly extended, tends to begin with the assumption that possibilities are unlimited by such lower-order conditions. Shortcomings in logic on either side look like gratuitous errors in ethics to the other. The logical mistake in either case is a failure to see the true "necessary condition" relations that hold; the result is in fact an unintended failure to maximize value; but the cause is ignorance, not vice.

28. A. N. Whitehead, chap. 13 in *Science and the Modern World* (New York, 1925).

29. The analogy of medicine and law is developed in Plato's *Gorgias*, though it certainly is earlier in inception. Underlying it is the danger of identifying a human *self* or *soul* with a physical organ — a Homeric *"aer"* or a modern neurological switchboard of tangled circuitry.

30. The I I I pattern for education is clearly best. But this fact may be hidden if one forgets that full self-realization requires social effectiveness and physical competence, as well as positive attitude. The notion of the superiority of an individual tutor to a larger school recognized the I I I pattern as an ideal, but overlooked the need for *S* and *E* values as conditions of its effective realization.

31. Hartman's theory (see above, n. 13) provided only for successively higher orders of "valuing." The resulting axiological analysis, as illustrated in the treatment of the opening pages of Plato's *Euthyphro* in *The Structure of Value*, quickly outruns the computational resources of even the most powerful modern computer.

32. I approve of descriptive comparisons of value, as well as normative appraisals; see above, n. 9.

Chapter 7 Metaphysical Systems

This chapter draws upon my article "Metaphysical Presuppositions and the Study of Time," originally published in *Proceedings* by Springer Verlag 1978, 1–22.

1. The "Divided Line" is a diagram introduced by Plato in *Republic* 6 to indicate different kinds and degrees of accuracy of "knowing." Its four levels run from myth and sheer conjecture (*eikasia*), on the lowest level, through a kind of "know-how" stage of arts and technique (*pistis*), then through a level of general hypothetical-deductive explanation (*dianoia*), to a final grasp of complete systems (*noesis*). These four types of knowing also represent successive stages of learning. See, on this point, my "The Divided Line and the

Direction of Inquiry," *Phil, Forum* 2 (1970–71): 172–99; "A New Interpretation of Plato's *Republic*," *Journal of Philosophy* 54 (1967): 661—70.

2. See my "Preface to Cosmography," *Review of Metaphysics* 7 (1952–53): 529–34; "Cosmography," *Review of Metaphysics* 25 (1971): 140–48; "Cosmography: The Problem of Modern Systems," *Review of Metaphysics* 26 (1973): 511–21.

3. Richard P. McKeon, *Freedom and History*(New York, 1952); Paul Weiss, *Modes of Being* (Carbondale, Ill., 1958); Plato, *Sophist* 246–51; Stallknecht and Brumbaugh, *The Compass of Philosophy*.

4. Stephan Körner, *Categorical Frameworks* (Oxford, 1970).

5. Newton P. Stallknecht and R. S. Brumbaugh, *The Spirit of Western Philosophy* (New York, 1950), xi-xvi.

6. See chap. 1, above.

7. J. T. Fraser, *Time as Conflict* (Basel, 1978).

8. The work of Franz Kafka is reprinted from *The Castle*, Definitive Edition, Trans. Ed. and W. Muir (New York: Alfred Knopf, 1941).

9. The work of Sophocles is reprinted from *Oedipus Rex*. Trans. by D. Storr (London and New York: Loeb Classical Library, 1934).

10. Henri Bergson, *Time and Free Will*, trans. F. L. Pogson (London, 1920).

11. The work of Thomas Mann is reprinted from *The Magic Mountain*, trans. H.T. Lowe-Porter (New York: Alfred A. Knopf, 1939).

12. For the "arrow" see H. D. P. Lee, *Zeno of Elea* (Cambridge, 1936); also "Zeno's Paradoxes of Motion," discussion in *The Philosophy of Time*, ed., Richard Gale New York, 1967), 387–494.

13. Georges Poulet, *Studies in Human Time*, trans. Eliot Coleman (Baltimore, 1956).

14. The work of Marcel Proust is reprinted from *Remembrance of Things Past*. Trans. by C. Scott Moncrieff (New York: Pantheon, 1928).

15. See above, chap. 5 pt. 2.

16. Weiss, *Modes of Being*.

Chapter 8. Systems and Tenses

This chapter draws upon my article "Systems, Tenses and Choices," originally published in *Midwestern Journal of Philosophy* (Murray State College) 1975, 9–14.

1. Cf. Sartre, *Existentialism*.

2. G. K. Plochmann, "The Cross That Bears Philosophy," *Midwestern Journal of Philosophy* 2 (Winter 1974): 24–38.

3. T. S. Kuhn, *The Structure of Scientific Revolutions* (Chicago, 1962); R. Hanson, *Patterns of Discovery* (Cambridge, 1958); S. Toulmin, *The Philosophy of Science* (New York, 1953); C. Kordig, *The Justification of Scientific Change* (Dordrecht, Holland, 1971).

4. R. Carnap. *The Logical Syntax of Language* (New York, 1937); C. G. Hempel, *Fundamentals of Concept Formation in Empirical Science* (Chicago, 1952).

5. S. Körner, *Categorical Frameworks*.

6. In particular, Gorgias's speech "On Nature" is an archetype of this skeptical approach; Sextus Empiricus offers another classical example.

7. The trouble is that the conjunction of all propositions true in more than one framework constitutes a contradiction. See my "Cosmography: The Problem of Modern Systems," 511–21.

8. Stallknecht and Brumbaugh, *The Compass of Philosophy*; my review of *Freedom and History* by R. P. McKeon, *Journal of Philosophy* (1954): 531–33.

9. See above, n. 7.

10. Kant's critical philosophy ends the modern attempts at a timeless synthesis. The next set of attempts are "Hegelian" in that the introduction of time is used to modify the application of the law of contradiction.

11. Plochmann, "The Cross That Bears Philosophy."

12. Stallknecht and Brumbaugh, *The Compass of Philosophy*.

13. Above, n. 5.

14. Above, n. 8.

Chapter 9. All Mixed Together

1. Plato, *Statesman* 273D5 ("Ocean of otherness," Simplicius, Proclus; "Place of otherness," MSS).

2. "Oh Sages burning in God's holy fire/ As in the gold mosaic on a wall..." W. B. Yeats, "Sailing to Byzantium."

3. Stephen Pepper, *World Hypotheses* (Berkeley, 1947); J. T. Fraser, *Time as Conflict* (Basel, 1978).

4. John Galsworthy, *The Forsythe Saga* (New York, 1921); A. Toynbee, *A Study of History* (New York and London, 1954); B. Franklin, *Autobiography* (London, 1905); W. McNeill, *The Rise of the West* (Chicago, 1963).

5. Aristotle's philosophy is throughout influenced by the paradigm of biological life cycles; a point generally recognized; but he himself does not use this metaphor very often. See. S. Pepper, *World Hypotheses* (Berkeley, 1947).

6. For *Oedipus Rex* and its time as crisis, see above, chap. 2; Aristotle, *Physics* 2. 194a26–30: "That is why the poet was carried away into making an absurd statement when he said 'he has the end for which he was born' [i.e., death]. For not every stage that is last claims to be an end, but only that which is best." Oxford trans.

7. See S. Macey, "The Changing Iconography of Father Time," International Society for the Study of Time, *Proceedings* 3 (1978): 540–75; and F. H. Haber's "Discussion and Comment," Ibid., 576–77. Also, the reproduction and comments on Brueghel's "The Triumph of Time," Frontispiece and Notes in J. T. Fraser, *The Voices of Time* (New York, 1966).

8. The fragments—carefully presented without intruded interpretative ordering—in Diels-Kranz, *Fragmente*. See P. Wheelwright, *Heraclitus* (Princeton, 1959) for a literary critic's interpretation; G. Kirk, *Heraclitus: The Cosmic Fragments* (Cambridge, 1954) for a controversial alternative. Also my *The Philosophers of Greece* (reissue, Albany, 1981), 43–50.

9. Just as examples, we can associate these with illustrative authors. River: Heralitus, Hesse, Mark Twain; Chariot: Marvel, Brueghel; Ship: Melville, Homer (*Odyssey*); Arrow: Zeno; Motorcycle: Pirsig (*Zen and the Art of Motorcycle Maintenance* [New York, 1974]).

10. A. N. Whitehead, *Process and Reality* (New York, 1929); *Science and the Modern World* (New York, 1925). Stephan Körner, *Abstraction in Science and Ethics* (London, 1971). See also my *Whitehead, Process Philosophy, and Education*, 37–85.

11. For the lantern slide image, see chap. 9, above. Also G. Poulet, *Studies in Human Time*, trans. E. Coleman (Baltimore, 1956).

12. The familiar train window is cited by Whitehead in a discussion of congruent ("cogredient") and different ("tilted") time systems in *The Concept of Nature*. See my *Whitehead, Process Philosophy, and Education*, 86ff. Above, n. 26, chap. 5, "Passage."

13. It is not clear where the current developments of quantum theory are headed. It is, however, a common project they share to "quantize" time. How this runs into Zeno's paradoxes depends on the strategy chosen, but it is not easy to get around them. See H. D. P. Lee, *Zeno of Elea* (Cambridge, 1936); Richard Gale, *The Philosophy of Time* (London, 1968), 387–502; my *The Philosophers of Greece*, 59–68.

14. J. T. Fraser, *Time as Conflict* (Basel, 1978)); also *Of Time, Passion, and Knowledge* (New York, 1975).

15. Joseph Conrad, *Heart of Darkness* (London, 1903).

16. Plato, *Symposium*, particularly 207A–211B.

17. H. Diels and W. Kranz, *Fragmente der Vorsokratiker*, Anaxagoras A1, II, p. 6 (Diogenes Laertius II 7; trans. R. D. Hicks [New York and London], I, 137.)

18. *Republic* 9. 592B1.

19. The ubiquitous lottery, unpredictable (hence uncaused) atomic swerve, and modern "random" music have some essential qualities in common. One of these is discussed in my "Notes on Art, Aesthetics, and Form," *Par Rapport* 1 (1978): 23–25.

20. Diels-Kranz *Frag.* 1, vol. 1, p. 89: *didonai gar auta dikēn kai tisin allēlois tēs kata tēn tou chronou taxin* ("paying penalties to one another according to the order of time").

Index

time as: complex causal nexus, 122; clock time, 134; deviation from pure form, 139; eternal backdrop, 15; field, 132–133; flow: rivers and fire, 133; framed static moments, 134; growth and natural cycle, 133; magic lantern slides, 134; metaphor, 136; process, 18; seen by poets, 140; transformation, 116
time in: Aristotle's practical sciences, 116–117; art, 5; Kafka's *The Castle*, 112–115; Mann's *The Magic Mountain*, 117–119; Proust's *Swann's Way*, 119–121; relation to pattern, process, and space, 138; Sophocles' *Oedipus Rex*, 115–117
topological properties of time, 46
transfinite numbers 88–89, 152nn10,11,12, 153n13
transformation, time as, 136
transformations relating philosophic systems 125
transposition of value orders, 96
trivial choices 90, 152n9
truth: tables 58; values, algebra of, 57, 151n27; values, changes of with time, 75, 151n36
Toulmin, S. 127, 155n3(ch8)
twentieth century obsession with time 9

unreality 3, 5, 45–55

value: change with time, 83–102; comparison, 91–92; extrinsic,

92–94; intrinsic, 94–95; levels of, 87; measures of, 86; orders and their transpositions, 96; patterns relating to choices, 101; systemic, 92; theory and intuitive notions of "better than", 84
values: and choices, 139; arithmetical model of, 84–85
Vienna Clock Museum, 28

W-observer 18–19, 145n4
Weiss, P. 109, 122, 154n13, 156n16
Wells Cathederal Clock 28
Whitehead, A.N.: 4, 9, 13, 17–18, 19–20, 23, 27, 30, 60,69, 144nn2,4,5,6,7,9, 145n12, 150nn3,5,11, 151nn28,31, 38, 154n28, 157n10
Whitehead and Russell 139
Whitehead on propositions 57–58, 76, 139
Whitehead's: analysis of problems of modern world, 63; ages of civilization, 22; phases of concrescence, 22; stages of learning, 22
Wilson, J. Cook 35, 146n15
world-soul, ratios of 37
Wordsworth, W. 19

Yeats, W.B. 156n2

Zen Buddhist 134
Zeno's: arrow 119; paradoxes, 134, 156n13
Zorba 117